Property of
TOMPKINS - CORTLAND
Community College

D1088440

PEOPLES OF THE EARTH

volume 1 Australia and Melanesia (including New Guinea)

volume 2 Africa from the Sahara to the Zambesi

volume 3 Europe (including USSR west of the Urals)

volume 4 Mexico and Central America

volume 5 Islands of the Atlantic (including the Caribbean)

volume 6 Amazonia, Orinoco and pampas

volume 7 Andes

volume 8 The Pacific – Polynesia and Micronesia

volume 9 Southern Africa and Madagascar

volume 10 Indonesia, Philippines and Malaysia

volume 11 South-East Asia

volume 12 The Indian subcontinent (including Ceylon)

volume 13 China (including Tibet), Japan and Korea

volume 14 USSR east of the Urals

volume 15 Western and central Asia

volume 16 The Arctic

volume 17 The Arab World

volume 18 North America

volume 19 Man the craftsman

volume 20 The Future of Mankind. General Index

volume ten

Indonesia Philippines and Malaysia

THE DANBURY PRESS

(Preceding page) Only 150 years ago Singapore was a quiet swampy island where 100 or so fishermen lived slow simple lives. Now it is the fourth busiest port in the world, and buildings and boats and people all jostle with each other for a little space to breathe.

Editorial Director **Tom Stacey**

Picture Director **Alexander Low**
Executive Editor **Katherine Ivens**
Art Director **Tom Deas**
Assistant Editor **Elisabeth Meakin**
Project Co-ordinator **Anne Harrison**
Research **Cheryl Moyer**

Specialist Picture Researcher **Elly Beintema**
Picture Research **Claire Baines**
Diana Eggitt
Jeanne Griffiths
Emma Stacey
Editorial Assistants **Richard Carlisle**
Rosamund Ellis
J M Marrin
Susan Rutherford
Pamela Tubby
Design Assistants **Susan Forster**
Richard Kelly
Cartography **Ron Hayward**
Illustrations **Sandra Archibald, Ron McTrusty**

Production **Roger Multon**
Production Editor **Vanessa Charles**

The publishers gratefully acknowledge help from the following organizations:
Royal Anthropological Institute, London
Musée de l'Homme, Paris
International African Institute, London
British Museum, London
Royal Geographical Society, London
Scott Polar Research Institute, Cambridge
Royal Asiatic Society, London
Royal Central Asian Society, London
Pitt-Rivers Museum, Oxford
Horniman Museum, London
Institute of Latin American Studies, London

PHOTOGRAPHIC CREDITS

Cover – **Burt Glinn** (Magnum from the John Hillelson Agency). 2, 3 and 14 through 23 – **Burt Glinn** (Magnum from the John Hillelson Agency) exc. bot. lt. 20 – **Mario de Biasi** (Epoca). 24 – **Ivan Polunin**. 25 – **Burt Glinn** (Magnum from the John Hillelson Agency). 26, 27 – **Dan McCoy** (Black Star, New York), **Burt Glinn** (Magnum from the John Hillelson Agency). 28 through 35 – **Robert Cundy**. 38 through 49 – **John Nance** (Magnum from the John Hillelson Agency). 50 through 53 – **F.P.G.** 54 through 65 – **Raghubir Singh** and **Anne de Henning** (The John Hillelson Agency). 66, 67 – **Ted Spiegel** (The John Hillelson Agency). 68 – **Romeo Vitug** (Black Star, New York), **William Hubbell** (F.P.G.). 69 through 72 – **Ted Spiegel** (The John Hillelson Agency). 73 – **William Hubbell** (F.P.G.). 74 – **Paul Popper**. 75 through 79 – **Hans Samsom**. 80 through 82 – **Ivan Polunin**. 82, 83 – **Hans Samsom**. 84 through 87 – **Anne de Henning** (The John Hillelson Agency) exc. bot. rt. 87 – **Jorgen Bitsch**. 88, 89 – **Victor Englebert, Anne de Henning** (The John Hillelson Agency). 90 – Black Star, London. 91 – **Anne de Henning** (The John Hillelson Agency). 92 through 94 – **Victor Englebert**. 95 – **C.H.M. Nooy-Palm, Anne de Henning** (The John Hillelson Agency). 96 – **Victor Englebert**. 97 – **Hans Samsom**. 98, 99 – **Victor Englebert**, (Susan Griggs). 100, 101 – **Hans Samsom**. 102 – **Burt Glinn** (Magnum from the John Hillelson Agency). 103 – **Hans Samsom, Litrau** (Paris Match). 105 – **Hans Samsom, Thomas Höpker** (The John Hillelson Agency). 106 – **Le Tac** (Paris Match). 107 through 109 – **Hans Samsom**, exc. top rt. 107 – **Burt Glinn** (Magnum from the John Hillelson Agency). 110, 111 – **Burt Glinn** (Magnum from the John Hillelson Agency). 112, 113 – **Ken Heyman**. 114 – **Burt Glinn** (Magnum from the John Hillelson Agency), **Hans Samsom, Mark Hobart**. 115 – **Burt Glinn** (Magnum from the John Hillelson Agency). 116 – **Henri Cartier Bresson** (Magnum from the John Hillelson Agency). 117 – **Ken Heyman**. 118, 119 – **Burt Glinn** (Magnum from the John Hillelson Agency), exc. bot. rt. 119 – **Anne de Henning** (The John Hillelson Agency). 120 through 122 – **Hans Samsom**. 123 – **Pascal Grellety-Bosviel, Mark Hobart, Hans Samsom**. 124 through 131 – **J. Rousseau**.

The Danbury Press
a division of Grolier Enterprises Inc.

Publisher
ROBERT B. CLARKE

Library of Congress Catalog Card No. 72 85614

Printed in Italy by
Arnoldo Mondadori Editore, Verona

Contents

Supervisory Editor of the Series:
Professor Sir Edward Evans-Pritchard,
Fellow of All Souls, Professor of Social Anthropology,
University of Oxford, 1946-1970,
Chevalier de la Légion d'Honneur

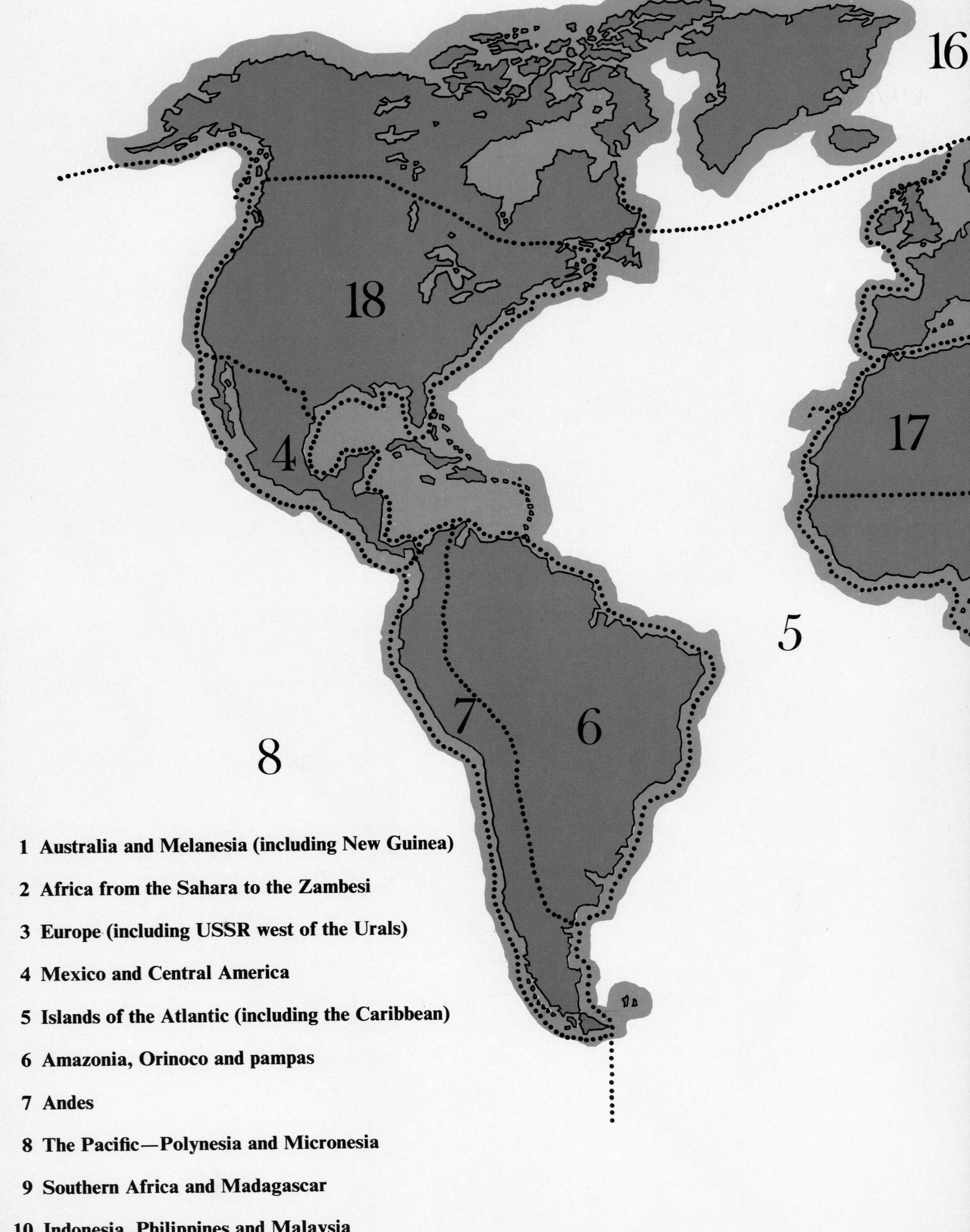
16
18
17
4
5
7
6
8
1 Australia and Melanesia (including New Guinea)
2 Africa from the Sahara to the Zambesi
3 Europe (including USSR west of the Urals)
4 Mexico and Central America
5 Islands of the Atlantic (including the Caribbean)
6 Amazonia, Orinoco and pampas
7 Andes
8 The Pacific—Polynesia and Micronesia
9 Southern Africa and Madagascar
10 Indonesia, Philippines and Malaysia

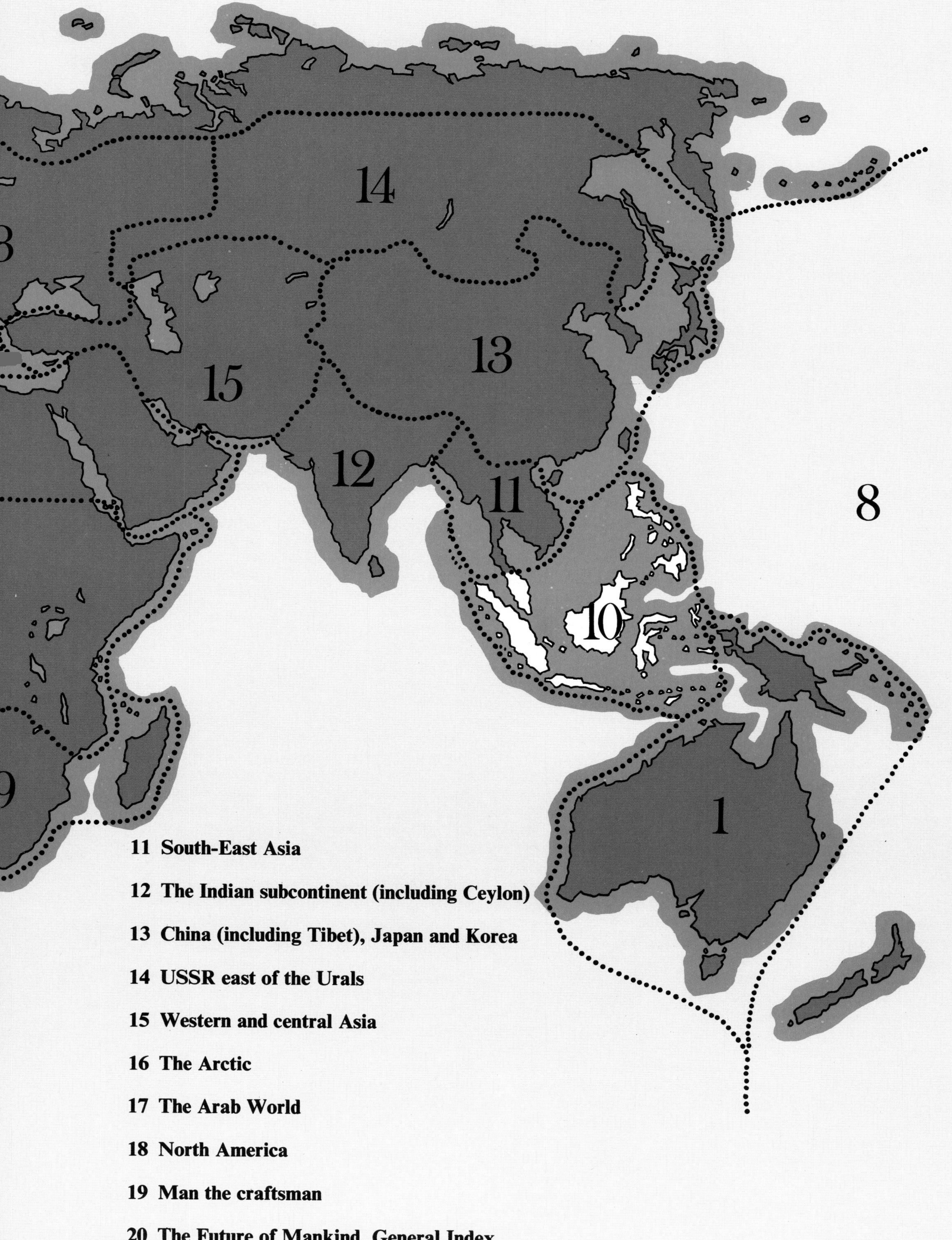
14
13
15
12
11
10
8
1

Man and his environment

Man began his career on the earth as apes in groups which varied in form and habits and fluctuated in numbers. Sometimes their number fell as low as a few thousand families. They became distinguished as our particular forbears by having a larger head, lighter build, straighter stance and smaller teeth than other apes. That was a little more than a hundred thousand of their and our generations ago. Can we tell anything about the environment they lived in at that remote period and what it meant to them?

The answer is that we can tell enough to make a start. The earliest men lived in tropical Africa in varying upland climates. Their world was more competitive than that of the great apes we know today. They had to compete for the food they needed with many neighbors and kindred stronger than themselves. They had to rely for their survival on quicker wits and readier invention. Their food was already diverse and became more so as they spread into new dwelling places or habitats. Their different tribes or races might be hunters or fowlers or fishers. With their mates they might also become collectors of plants or shell-fish or grubbers-up of insects. In these ways their environment provided them first with food, then with drugs and poisons, and with clothing.

This varied activity meant that man had to know in a practical way the animals and plants around him. He had to know where and when he could find them and what uses he could make of them. All these resources, and sources of water too, were liable to shift or fail dangerously. Beyond this older knowledge he was in the process of discovering that wood and horn and bone could be fashioned into tools and weapons, and that different kinds of stone, skilfully treated, could give him even more effective instruments of attack and defense. From being merely a botanist and a zoologist he was becoming a geologist and a mechanic, and his success in planning his work was bound to have carried with it a new and more confident attitude towards time and space, and towards understanding the operations of cause and effect in the world around him.

These new instruments and the new faculties or intelligence which had invented them accompanied the growth of his brain. It favored the survival of the inventors and their descendants and thus favored development of a more complicated brain, and of further invention. It also set him on the course of multiplying his numbers and expanding the territory in which he lived. From a few thousands he came to be a few millions. From being an African he came to occupy first Europe and Asia, then America and Australia. Finally by his skill in boat building and star watching he was able to occupy the remotest islands of the Pacific so that the sea as well as the land became the environment of a new Polynesian breed of navigators.

With each new advance man was evidently diversifying his environments. And peoples who were living in different environments had different opportunities and were of necessity selected divergently for their ability to make the most of them. They produced different geographical races which survived only when they fitted the different climates and different ways of living. Peoples in colder climates lost the color in their skin and even in their hair and their eyes. People in warmer climates became even darker and lost their body hair completely. In the open they became taller but in deep forest they often became shorter, like the many races of pygmies we see today. In the Arctic they became broader and fatter like the Eskimo who survives on the ice, feeding almost solely on meat. Most remarkable of all were the people who made their way up to the tablelands of Tibet and of Bolivia at heights of 12,000 feet and more, who then developed larger lungs and redder blood. Fitness for one environment however usually entails unfitness for another. The lowlanders find life hard in the highlands. But the highlanders are liable to die of tuberculosis if they are brought down to the lowlands.

Different kinds of people and different races are thus prevented from mixing not only by the more obvious mountains and oceans, and mere distances that separate them, but also by their mental and physical adaptations to different environments. As for distance, through most of his history man could probably not shift his habitat much faster than a mile a year. He seems to have needed 8,000 years to cover the 8,000 miles from the Bering Strait to Tierra del Fuego.

Why did he move so slowly? He was moving across country with a vast supply, an unlimited supply as it must have seemed to him, of game and grain and roots and fruits. But the character of these supplies changed with the land and the climate. And for each change the Amerindian, as we call him, had to change his habits, his skills and his inborn character. He made his journey right across the tropics. He went slowly because it was an evolutionary journey. But at the end of his journey we notice that his skin had never become as dark as the color of the negro or Melanesian of the Old World. It was only when African negroes were brought to America after Columbus that black skin color appeared in the New World.

The narrow range of skin colors in the New as compared with the Old World teaches us several useful lessons. First, it shows us that skin color represents an extremely stable characteristic or marker of races. Then it shows us that such characteristics change only when there are hereditary changes or mutations in a race; and that these changes are so rare that they never occurred in the roughly thousand-generation history of the population of America. Finally, it shows us that as with the other hereditary changes, there is no direct effect of the environment. Sunburn will not change the skin color of a race. What it will do is to produce skin cancer in the pale-skinned individual and so, by natural selection, favor the survival, when there are any, of darker individuals in the population.

Not only expansion of numbers and need for more space but also a second factor, change of climate, has led to great movements of peoples. During the latter half of man's history there have been four great ice ages. Each of these has been followed by a warm spell such as we are now enjoying. There has then been a melting of the caps of ice around the poles, a rise in the level of the oceans, with the flooding of vast areas of land, and a shift in the rain and desert belts which girdle the earth. All these changes spread over a few thousand years forced men to move back and forth in search of better, or more accustomed conditions above all in search of food. It was the last of these worldwide movements which is connected with a great revolution in human affairs: the establishment of agriculture simultaneously in the Old and in the New World.

Environmental conditions had a decisive influence in determining the time and place of this revolution. For it happened just when the ice was retreating fastest, some 10,000 years ago. It happened at places with a temperate climate, in the Fertile Crescent, as we call it, on the highland northward edge of Arabia, and in the highlands of Mexico and Peru. A glance at the map shows us that these regions lie in very special positions on the earth's surface, next to narrow necks of land joining continents where men in movement were compelled to meet and to mix. These bottlenecks were moreover places where plants grew wild which could provide the grains and the pulses, the oils and the fibers needed to establish fixed and self-supporting settlements of cultivators. There were two entirely different sets of crop plants grouped around wheat in the Old World, and round maize in the New.

Even with these favorable conditions the first cultivators, we find, had no easy task or quick success. They had previously been collecting wild wheat and barley grain on poor hillsides and storing it over winter for food. Now they scratched the earth, sowed grain that they had saved, and waited to harvest it. By selection, over several millennia, they turned their wild grain into a cultivated crop. It was an unconscious selection for they could not have forseen what the result would be. Slowly they learnt that they could use their grain to feed cattle and use the cattle to plow deeper soils, and use both grain and cattle to feed people; not only themselves but also a swelling band of craftsmen and traders, who were drawn in from far afield to help them. Slowly, with this help and their secure supply of food, they learnt how to build terraces and canals, to design towns and cities, and to site them in relation to the earth and water and vegetation they needed.

This work was nothing less than the business of establishing civilization and it occupied its pioneers in and around Mesopotamia for four millennia and in the New World, where there were no cattle, perhaps even longer. During a hundred generations or more, our ancestors had transformed both themselves and their environment. They had brought their environment, which had been 'nature', under their control so that it was no longer merely nature. And they, or at least their kings and priests, gradually became aware of what had happened and were (as their inscriptions show) inclined to boast of their achievement.

Part of this achievement meant that men were now divided in new ways by the new activities they had invented. Beneath it all there was the contrast, the hereditary opposition between the peasant and the herdsman who were dependent on, and therefore adapted to, the two kinds of environment they had created. The one was patient, prudent, industrious and attached to the soil and the crops which he knew and possessed, loved and even worshipped. The other was adventurous, energetic, nomadic and attached to the sheep, cattle or horses which he equally possessed and equally worshipped. Each depended for his survival on his skill in understanding the means of his livelihood, which was the kind of domesticated farming he and his people had made feasible and fruitful. For this reason different kinds of people, as the story of Cain and Abel shows, were often in conflict.

Evidently the new domesticated people had gained much by their evolution but they had also lost some of their skills and versatility, and with them some of the independence of the hunter and collector. Each class of civilized people had become dependent on the specialized materials they used and the complicated societies which they had developed and of which they now formed a part. Those societies were beginning to constitute environments for new kinds of men in which each class of man follows its own hereditary trade or profession and feels at home in it. This process of stratification in the environment is also a process of evolution and it is still going on today in all advanced or advancing societies.

There was yet another consequence of farming which came from the denser populations that grew up when rich land came under the plow. We know of it from the rules that priests drew up to protect the health of their people. We know of it also from the account *Exodus* gives us of the plagues of Egypt, including infectious diseases of a kind which are still the bane of men and cattle in most tropical and subtropical lands. The closer people and cattle live together the more they are liable to be infected by plagues. But when people have been exposed to such diseases the survivors are often found to be resistant to them. Natural selection has changed the character of each race to suit its own local environment of disease.

The disease element in the environment, the part that

man for long failed to control, proved to be, after the invention of agriculture, an additional and most decisive factor governing the movements and migrations of peoples. It took effect in two ways. On the one hand the heavier price may be paid by the migrant: the Europeans, for example, who encountered malaria and yellow fever in West Africa – diseases which kept the Europeans and their civilization out of Africa until the present century. On the other hand, the greater damage may be inflicted by the migrant: the Europeans, for example, who took their smallpox and measles with them to America and to Polynesia, and killed off great numbers of the native peoples whenever they made contact. Indeed it was from noticing this result in West Africa at the beginning of the 19th century, that an English physician, Dr W C Wells, first arrived at the principle which Darwin was to make famous under the name of natural selection.

What happened in this regard in South America constitutes one of man's most notable, although again unconscious experiments with his environment. The Amerindians entering this continent had been twice filtered or screened in their separation and isolation from the rest of mankind: once through the Bering Strait and once through the Isthmus of Panama. They are in consequence – and their blood groups show it – the most homogenous people, the purest of the great races in the world. And they also proved to be the most susceptible of all native people to European diseases. The North American Indians were devastated by gunpowder. The South Americans were destroyed even more by disease. To this rule there were two exceptions: those groups which were protected by their special isolation and adaptation in Andean tablelands and in tropical jungles; and those groups which were protected by hybridization with Europeans or Africans. The shanty towns around South America's capital cities are occupied solely by hybrids and by intruders, the mestizo, the mulatto and the African negro. The pure Amerindian has never been able to survive in the cities of other peoples.

There is one other aspect of this great human experiment. The Amerindian does not or cannot go into the cities. The negro does not or cannot go into the highlands. Have they allowed the environment to select them? Or have they used their intelligence to select their environment? The relative importance of the two courses of events must vary with the place and the people. But the history of the slave trade shows us yet another factor in propagation and survival. For the Muslim Arabs took the negroes from Africa to be used and discarded. The Christian Europeans took them from Africa to be used and bred: whence the presence of many millions of negroes in America and their near absence in Asia.

There is one last notable consequence of man's tendency to take control of his environment. It is the consequence of his short-sightedness. He is, to be sure more farsighted than any other animal, but he has often, increasingly often, allowed himself to exhaust or destroy for his immediate profit just those things around him which he has found most readily available. The temptation to improve his standard of living has been irresistible. What has led him to this disastrous course?

We can trace back to very early times opposing policies governing man's habit of damaging his environment. Most primitive hunters avoid killing off the prey on which they depend. Even in catching hedgehogs our Gypsies respect a closed breeding season. And primitive people limit their own population by infanticide, abortion or delayed sexual initiation. But it seems that any successful new invention was liable to break down this calculated or instinctive restraint. In Africa 50,000 years ago a new weapon, the hand axe, enabled hunters to kill off many African game animals. Much later, when the Amerindians – equipped with their newly invented bow – broke across the Bering Strait and found themselves surrounded by unlimited herds, again the temptation to kill was irresistible. And in destroying whole species its results were irremediable.

The inventions, in modern times, of fire-arms, the factory ship and the explosive harpoon for killing whales are in a direct line of descent from these earlier technical exploits, and they are today having even more devastating consequences for the animal resources of the earth. Less direct and more complex however are the developments in the practice of agriculture itself.

When the earliest cultivators cut down the forest – sparing the fruit trees – and hoed the hillsides to sow their seed, they noticed that the rain washed away the soil. So they built terraces and conduits to save the seed, the soil and the water. Later they replanted the forest with orchards and vineyards which they fenced off from cattle and pigs. But when the herdsman appeared he burnt the forest; he let his sheep and goats graze and browse everywhere; he left the land ruined; and he moved on elsewhere. In later ages he often came back and, inspired by Muslim or another war-like faith, he turned the villages and terraces, conduits and canals of the cultivator into a desert from which there was to be no recovery.

Thus some men have treated their environments with respect for the future. Others, especially in war, have taken no account of the future. But the most stable conditions in the world, inspired by Hinduism and little disturbed by any of our European passion for progress, have led to repeated disaster in India. There, men and cattle have both propagated without limit, The timber and the grassland has been used up in the interests of the cattle, and the cow dung, which could have been used to restore the fertility of the soil, has been regularly burnt for fuel.

So much for Islam and Hinduism. But Christianity can scarcely claim to have done better. It has inspired a belief in unlimited progress, based on an unlimited superiority of man over nature, and a consequent increasing disregard for the restraints imposed on man in primitive society. Where population has been restricted it has only been with the purpose of competing in extravagance, of wasting all the resources that nature has provided. And the effect, as it now appears, is to poison the earth, the air and the water, and in general to diminish the by no means infinite future prospects of life.

What we can now see of our relations with our environment tells us that we have to look at it and at ourselves from a new point of view. It is no longer possible for men, or the rulers of men, to say with the confidence of an earlier generation that they are in control of their environment or of nature. By a strange paradox, our own inventions have taken control both of the earth and of us. We have become increasingly the property of our own possessions. It is they as much as we who plan our existence and decide our future. We no longer stand apart from them. We are swallowed up in them.

The great connection of man with his environment, and the long history of his endeavors which has led up to it, is thus something that we can partly understand. Partly, because we can read and write. But in mankind we have to include simpler people than ourselves. The Bushman, the Negrito, and the Aborigine can hardly understand anything of this. The Eskimo hunter and the Masai herdsman (like the dwellers in the shanty towns) can understand all too little. Unless we protect these simpler peoples many are likely to disappear, and if they do so they will be as much the victims of our civilized environment as are the gazelles of the desert and the whales of the deep sea.

Peoples of Malaysia

Appearances can be deceptive in Malaysia. The luxuriant vegetation of the tropical forests belies the general poverty of the soil and although the different races – Malay, Chinese, and Indian – seem calmly established, almost all they have in common is that they all eat rice as their staple food.

The races are concentrated in different areas, they follow different occupations, and they do not mix. They have no common social or linguistic ground except for English, and Malays cannot marry outside the Islamic faith.

Malays are now outnumbered by the combined Chinese and Indian populations—the result of successive waves of immigration to meet successive demands for labor: First the 'tin rush' brought Chinese to the western inland area late in the 19th century. Then, early in the 20th century, Indians came to work on the rubber plantations. The high rate of immigration, particularly of Chinese, continued until government restrictions were imposed in 1929. In Malaya, Sabah, and Sarawak over a third of the population is now Chinese. Nearly 40 per cent of the population in Sabah and Sarawak are indigenous Dayaks, who used to be ferocious headhunters. In Singapore over three-quarters are Chinese. About a tenth of the whole population is of Indian or Pakistani origin.

The Malays remain overwhelmingly a rural people and the *kampong* (village) with its palm-thatched wooden houses raised on piles is purely Malay in character. They fish, raise livestock, grow rice, coconuts, fruit and vegetables, and in this the other races have hardly ever competed with them. The Malays are particularly concentrated in the north and east, where good transport is a comparatively recent development and Chinese and Indian settlement is sparse. This emphasises the Chinese predominance in the western cities and Singapore.

Within the Chinese population the Hakka, Hainanese, Cantonese, Hokkien and Tiechiu speak different languages, eat different food, tend to have different occupations, and separate into distinct districts if they live in the same town. The Chinese have a prominent position in the commercial affairs of Malaysia and, with their growing numbers and increasing political influence, have often incurred Malay resentment.

The majority of Indians are Tamils from southern India, and do not show the same tendency to form separate communities. They are mainly traders and shopkeepers, and a few live in rural areas in the western states.

Malaysia is rich in tin deposits and the climate suits the rubber tree, but less than 20 per cent of the land is suitable for agriculture. Much of the central and northern peninsula is too steep for cultivation, or too swampy.

The very high humidity in Malaysia means that the average temperature of 75 degrees, which varies very little throughout the year, often feels suffocatingly hot. There is no real dry season. On the east coast the monsoon season is between late October and March. On the west coast it is between May and August, but it is not as regular or as pronounced. Singapore has no monsoon.

The earliest inhabitants of the peninsular were aboriginal groups from the Asian continent: Negroids (known in Malaya as Semang), Australoids (Semai-Temiar, sometimes classified as Senoi) and Proto-Malays (Jakun). When the ancestors of the Malays drifted down from Yunnan – probably between 2,500 and 1,500 BC – these aboriginal groups retreated to the highland forests where they remain. The Semang live mainly in the northern areas, the Semai-Temiar in the centre, and the Jakun in the south where some integrate with Malays.

Indian settlement in Malaysia began as early as the first century AD and Indian culture has had a strong influence on Malayan culture. The Malays adopted the Indian religions of Hinduism and Buddhism until their conversion to Islam, again introduced by Indians in the 15th century, and complete by the 17th century.

European cultural influence has always been slight. The Portuguese, who captured Malacca in 1511, and the Dutch, who took it from them in 1641, came in very small numbers and were interested only in trade. In spite of their missionary zeal the Portuguese failed to make any impression on the Malays. The English East India Company acquired the island of Penang in 1786 in exchange for protecting the Sultan of Kedah from the Siamese and the Burmese. Ten years later Malacca came under English control. In 1819 Singapore was founded and soon became the most important trading port in the east.

But Malaysia was not colonized by the British whose interest was confined to the three Straits Settlements, Penang, Malacca and Singapore, until civil wars in the peninsula threatened the future of the tin mines. In 1874 the British took over the protection of the Federated Malay States of Johore, Perak, Selangor, Negri Sembilan and Pahang. The four states of Kedah, Perlis, Kelantan and Trengganu remained independent until 1948.

Malaysia was occupied by the Japanese for three and a half years in World War II, and during this time the communist guerrilla forces in the highlands strengthened their popularity with the local people by constantly harassing the Japanese. So the stage was set for the communist 'Emergency' which began in 1948 and lasted for twelve years. Many people from remote areas were resettled in new villages away from communist influence, and tension between the races increased dangerously.

In 1963 the states of Sarawak, Sabah, Singapore, and Malaya achieved political unity as Malaysia. The union was short-lived and Singapore seceded in 1965, for the Singapore Chinese felt that their large share in producing the country's prosperity was not matched by their political power in the union. Once again, the root of the problem was racial feeling.

Malaysia is a relatively prosperous area, but the widely divergent interests of the different races poses an unsolved problem. Political unity seems impossible while racial boundaries are as real as national frontiers.

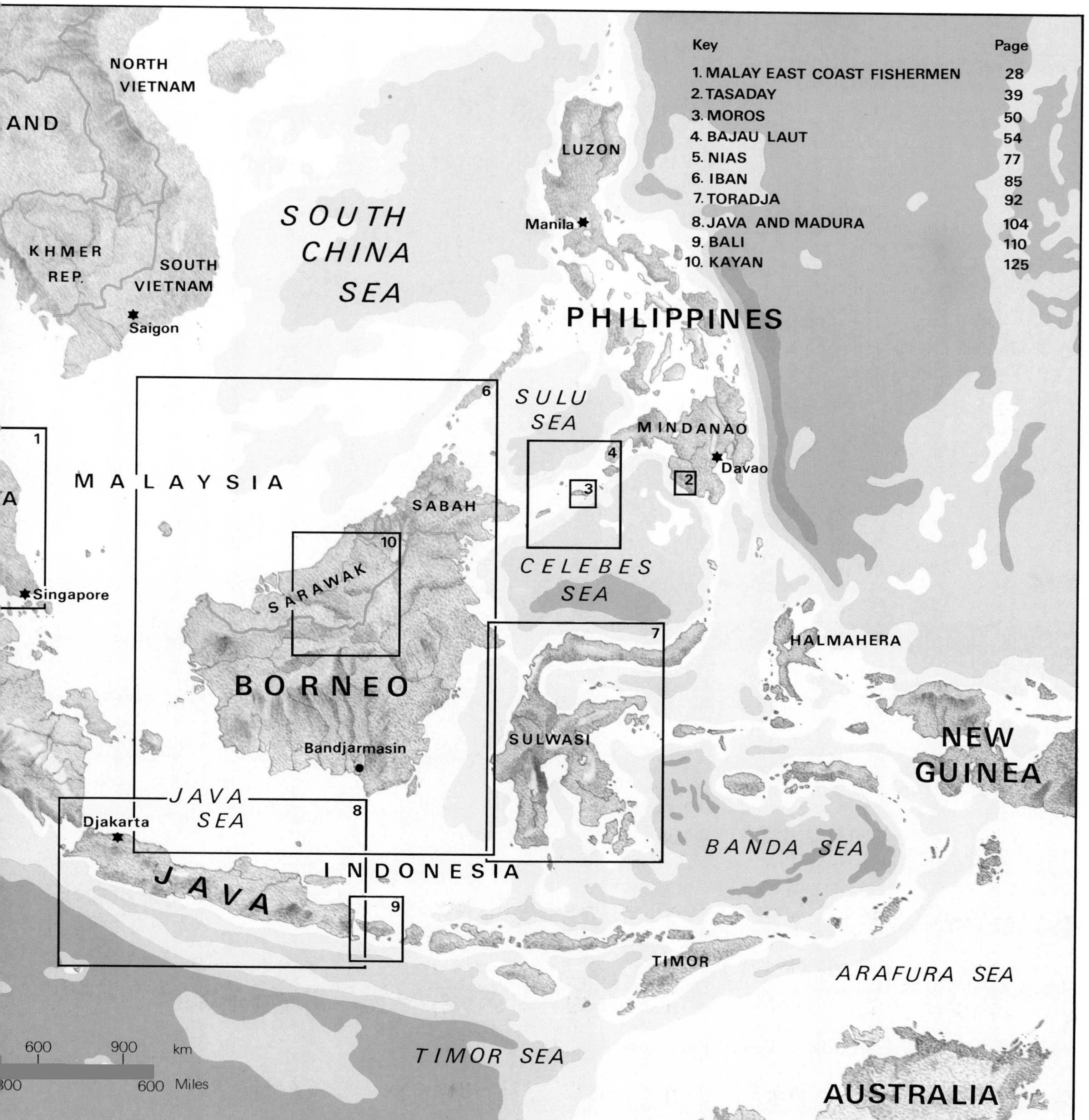
Key
Page
1. MALAY EAST COAST FISHERMEN 28
2. TASADAY 39
3. MOROS 50
4. BAJAU LAUT 54
5. NIAS 77
6. IBAN 85
7. TORADJA 92
8. JAVA AND MADURA 104
9. BALI 110
10. KAYAN 125
NORTH VIETNAM
AND
KHMER REP.
SOUTH VIETNAM
Saigon
SOUTH CHINA SEA
LUZON
Manila
PHILIPPINES
SULU SEA
MINDANAO
Davao
MALAYSIA
SABAH
Singapore
SARAWAK
CELEBES SEA
BORNEO
HALMAHERA
SULWASI
NEW GUINEA
Bandjarmasin
JAVA SEA
Djakarta
JAVA
INDONESIA
BANDA SEA
TIMOR
ARAFURA SEA
TIMOR SEA
AUSTRALIA
600 900 km
300 600 Miles

Chinese Singapore

In 1819 Singapore was nothing. Or rather, it was a swampy jungle island where just over a hundred people, most of them Malay fishermen, lived simple slow rugged lives far from the gaze of the outside world. But then came an adventurous British empire builder called Raffles. He liked the look of Singapore and thought it would make a fine commercial port, with strategic possibilities too. His idea was taken up, he was proved right within months, and he died years later as Sir Stamford Raffles, a famous man. But it was the Chinese who transformed the idea into reality.

Singapore is the fourth busiest port in the world, after New York, Rotterdam and Yokohama – and it may soon go up into third place. The average income of the inhabitants is, after Japan, the highest in Asia. Singapore is a by-word for prosperity, and the people who have made it prosperous are almost all Chinese. Some 75 per cent of the islanders of Singapore are Chinese in ancestry. Singapore is essentially Chinese.

Now the jungle has all been chopped down. There is little room for agriculture – most of the Singaporeans' food is imported. The island, shaped like a diamond with the sharp points at the west and eastern tips, lies at the very toe of the great Malayan peninsula, tenuously connected by a causeway across the Straits of Johore which separate Singapore from Malaya, now called Western Malaysia.

The island of Singapore is 26 miles west to east and 13 miles north to south. The hundred-odd population of 1819 has swollen to well over two million. The Chinese do indeed predominate, but there are also Arabs, Armenians, Jews, Cypriots, Ceylonese, and Sikhs from the Punjab. There are Eurasians, and Europeans of every nationality. And 14 per cent of Singaporeans are Malays, almost all of them Muslim. There are 8 per cent who are Indian in ancestry – most of them Tamils from southern India and Ceylon. In Singapore you can find most of the world's great religions, some of them so intermingled that you cannot categorize them. Tourists further swell the numbers and there are sailors from every nation. Singapore is at the crossroads of world maritime and air routes.

In the harbor you see every sort of vessel, from oil-tankers to junks, awkward but sturdy, and the flimsy *sampans* that take only a few agile passengers. And then there are the rickety-looking *kelongs* – large bamboo frames which Malay fishermen drag out into the sea and make into temporary fishing headquarters from which they hang traps and cast nets.

Go-downs (the local name for warehouses) stand at the water's edge, propping each other up. Shops find space to spring up anywhere. Old temples share their room with bus companies. And at the edge of the city, you see Malay-style wooden houses standing on stilts to avoid the swampiness of the wet season. (In fact there is no clear season in Singapore. Twenty miles north of the

Hueys, ruthless Chinese gangs, and the 'squeeze' go hand in hand with opium dens which a determined government has been unable to stamp out.

In 1819 a swampy island inhabited by a few Malay fishermen, Singapore is now the world's fourth busiest port with a population over 2 million.

equator, the weather is usually much the same: hot and humid, with the occasional cloudburst.) Towering above the makeshift conglomeration of dwellings stand gargantuan high-rise blocks, where 40 per cent of the population now live. There is a steady flow of families from the merry but not always hygienic *kampongs*, the old country villages that clustered on the edge of the city, to the new blocks. In Singapore the noise never stops. Nor do many of the factories where a large proportion of the Chinese now work.

The Chinese of Singapore are famous for their industriousness and determination. Many shopkeepers open up before eight in the morning and close down at ten in the evening. Everything is bustle.

But one and a half centuries ago all was quiet. The main island of Singapore and the fifty or so outlying islets saw just the occasional wooden boats of the Malays and of the Bugis, a fishing tribe who fished the waters nearby. Way back in the 7th century AD the Sumatran Srivijaya Empire made Singapore a trade center and called it Temasek (or Sea Town). The aboriginal inhabitants they called Orang Laut. But both they and the city had disappeared by the time Raffles appeared on the scene. Only the name was left behind, later anglicized to Singapore from Singapura (Hindi for Lion City), so called because a Sumatran prince who landed there in the 13th century saw an animal 'very swift and beautiful, its body bright red, its head jet black, its breast white, in size rather larger than a he-goat'. It was probably a tiger, but the prince's party called it a lion and gave the modern city its name.

Four months after Raffles formally set up a trading station at Singapore there were already over five thousand people. The island was rented, then bought outright, from the Sultan of Johore by the British East India Company, before becoming a Crown Colony in 1867. In the early days Malays and Chinese came in equal numbers, but by 1836 the Chinese had overtaken the Malays and they continued to pull away numerically from then on. They are now just over 75 per cent of the total populace. The Malays generally went into domestic service or government service. But the Chinese stuck firmly to business, and they soon controlled most of the mushrooming entrepôt trade, on which the economy is based, as well as the agriculture and pig rearing.

Not that the Chinese were homogeneous – far from it. They all came from southern China, but they spoke at least eight different languages. People from the same area usually stuck together and monopolized their own chosen sector of the economy. The Hylamese from the island of Hainan founded the restaurant trade, and dominated it. The Hokkiens, from Amoy and southern

Chinese junks, little changed in hundreds of years, find harbor space beside some of the largest and most modern ships in the world.

Some Malay villagers remain on the coast, but more and more families are moving into high-rise apartment blocks in the rapidly growing city.

An actor carefully applies make-up backstage before a *wayang* performance, highly stylized but popular Chinese opera.

Children have the best view in a crowded *wayang* theater; they are allowed to watch the performance sitting on the stage itself.

Fukien, who made up 40 per cent of the Chinese, went into general trade. The Cantonese, from south Kwangtung, formed 19 per cent and were almost all craftsmen. Even bicycle-making was a closed shop, open only to men from one particular area. Two tight-knit communities (7 per cent of the Chinese population) were the Hakhahs and the Kheks from north Kwangtung. Over a fifth of the Chinese were Teochews and Hoklos from eastern Kwangtung, while there were still other small groups each with their own language and identity: the Kwongsais from mid-Kwangsi and the Hokchias from Foochow and coastal mid-Fukien. Interprovincial marriage was frowned upon, if not actually forbidden. And despite the first stirrings of anti-colonial, mainly anti-British, feeling during the first Opium War of 1840 and later during the Boxer Rising in Peking at the turn of the century, the Chinese of Singapore were more concerned to make money than foment revolution. Conflict – often physical – erupted between the Chinese communities, not between the Chinese and the British.

The early leaders of the Chinese were the Babas. They were the descendants of the first Chinese arrivals and Malay women. Often known as the Straits Chinese, they were the first to make big money. Though never more than 10 per cent of the Chinese populace, they continued to have a strong influence until the 1940s, since when their customs have faded.

Sinologists often say that the Chinese are invariably clannish. If Singapore is anything to go by, this is so. Friction between those from different regions of China and between Babas and the rest soon manifested itself in the flowering of secret societies, called *hueys*, or brotherhoods. They sprang up wherever there were Chinese communities in the *Nan-Yang* (literally: southern ocean, but really anywhere between Burma and the Philippines). Originally founded to overthrow the decadent Manchu dynasty, the societies retained much of their religious symbolism but their purposes often became purely criminal. The fearsome Triad was once a purely political group, named after the *Thien-ti-hui*, the 'cosmic association' of human, terrestrial and celestial powers, which it was hoped would overthrow the Manchus. But it evolved into a protection gang. Some Singapore *hueys* would kidnap Chinese coolies in China and sell them to the agents in Singapore who arranged for the immigration of labor. Other *hueys* brought across brides. Everywhere they were masters of the 'squeeze', the Singapore name for graft. They operated inside the very temples which always attracted semi-religious hangers-on (like fortune-tellers) who could be 'squeezed'. Even the Christian Chinese, once persecuted, had to form a *huey*. The opium farms and the gambling dens were always bedevilled by *hueys*. And if you didn't *kow-tow* to them, as the expression went, life was rough.

There are claims that *hueys* today operate even within a trade union framework, although the authorities say

A family pose for a photograph in the Tiger Balm Gardens, one of two amusement parks built by heirs to a patent medicine fortune.

Singapore is a tiny island; each year more of its growing population move to government-built apartment blocks like this one.

Foreign visitors join ordinary shoppers in markets where a vigilant government has made sure that the city is the cleanest in Asia.

they have stamped out almost all *hueys*. Those that remain are slightly less bloody and have lost their aura of ritual. In the old days there was the *huey's* headman, backed by the Red Wand (his top thug), supported by five Tiger Generals and a Council of Twenty. The exotic names may have gone, but secret societies now have elaborate code names and code numbers instead.

Even if the *hueys* have faded, they have certainly left behind a strong tradition of clannishness, ruthlessness and acceptance of 'squeeze' as part of life. Provincial differences have faded too – you will only hear the old or the very conservative talking their provincial languages. Taboos forbidding people with the same family surname – Ong, Chan, Sun, for example – from marrying have gone out as well. Still, clannishness in many aspects of life, in business and in society, is especially noticeable among the Chinese of Singapore. Outsiders often find Chinese easier to talk to than the Malays – the Chinese are usually more sophisticated, quicker, and they are charming and cheerful too; but they say they are harder to make *real* friends with.

But there is a paradox here. The Chinese love to be together within a solid set. They like to crowd together to gamble or to eat or to smoke opium (though the government is assiduously stamping out the habit). Yet each man is expected to make his own way in the tough competitive life of the business-island. They are perhaps less possessive of privacy in matters like housing than westerners, yet they do not have the African-style concept of collective responsibility. They grow up to be strongly individualist.

Evening brings no peace to Bugis Street. It is closed to traffic, food-stalls are set up and the bustle goes on far into the night.

Traditional religion in Singapore is dying. Although there are over 400 temples in Singapore, their numbers are declining to make way for new buildings. Many of the Chinese are becoming Christian, usually Roman Catholic. But experts often claim that for the Chinese religion is much less ethereal, more functional than westerners think it to be. As the expert on Chinese temples put it: they are very 'This-Worldly'.

The religion that evolved among the Chinese Singaporeans was a unique amalgam of the three main Chinese religions – Taoism, Buddhism and Confucianism, the last more a code of behavior than a religion. There is a story that three sages were seen walking towards Merdeka Bridge. One was Confucius, another was Lao Tzu, founder of Taoism, the third was Amithabha, 'the Buddha that presides over the western paradise'. They were arguing for their respective creeds. Confucius pleaded for an end to the ills of society on this earth. Lao Tzu thought the problem insoluble and advocated anarchy. Amithabha urged them to prepare for Nirvana in the next world, the state of non-existence and perfect bliss. They crossed the bridge, but were lost in a rainstorm. When the rain lifted, only one man could be seen – unrecognizable as any of the original three. The moral is that in Singapore the various creeds merged.

Many gods are worshipped by both Taoists and Buddhists, and have acquired wholly Singaporean characters. Some temples have turned Confucius himself into a god. In Singapore, Kuan Yiu, goddess of mercy, who rejected Nirvana in order to comfort those on earth, has overtaken the Buddha himself in popularity. She is often known as the Third Aunt or the Bodhisattva. A favorite god is Kuan Tai or Kuan Kung, God of War. But he is chivalrous and defends the weak, as well as being the epitome of martial ferocity. Nine feet tall with a two-foot beard, he is the idol of literature as well as of numerous secret societies.

The temples – often built at the expense of a rich man – are sometimes simple, even dilapidated, sometimes grand. But they never have the strongly 'sacred' feel of Christian churches, though they are always full of candles, paper lanterns and incense offered by devotees. There are plenty of hangers-on, particularly mediums, who claim to be able to speak to your ancestors and intercede with the gods. You know if a temple has a medium by spotting the tools of his trade like the spike-chair, the knife-table, or the knife-ladder. When the

Malays now make up only 14 per cent of Singapore's population and many resent Chinese commercial and political power.

In front of Machokang temple a story-teller entertains an audience. Illiterate people, especially, often sit listening all evening.

medium sits, lies or climbs these respective objects, he mutilates himself. Sometimes he whips himself. A helper sprays water from his mouth onto the medium's wounds, then rubs in ashes.

Only the old people follow the old religions today, though there are some young Buddhists. Most progressive, ambitious Singaporeans are Christian or atheists, though most Malays and Tamils hold to their ancestors' beliefs. Chinese funerals are still slow processions, followed by large numbers of mourners clanging gongs, beating drums and wailing loudly. (In Malaysia, carping Malays sometimes say 'The living Chinese block the economy, while the dead block the traffic.') But today's weddings are usually quick registry-office ceremonies. Even in the old days, codes of behavior were *not* inextricably tangled with religious belief, as in the west. Few Chinese feel the need for a strong religion when Singapore, independent as part of Malaysia in 1963, then truly independent when it broke away from Malaysia in 1965, has built its own brand of strident nationalism. Nationalism, as invoked by the socialist but anti-communist premier, Lee Kuan Yew, is part of the life of every Singaporean (especially if he is Chinese, although this would be officially denied). The first fresh

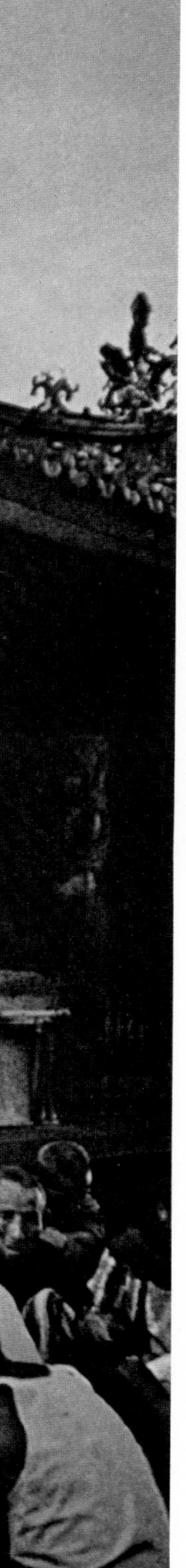

On this tough, competitive business island every enterprise must try to attract as many customers as possible.

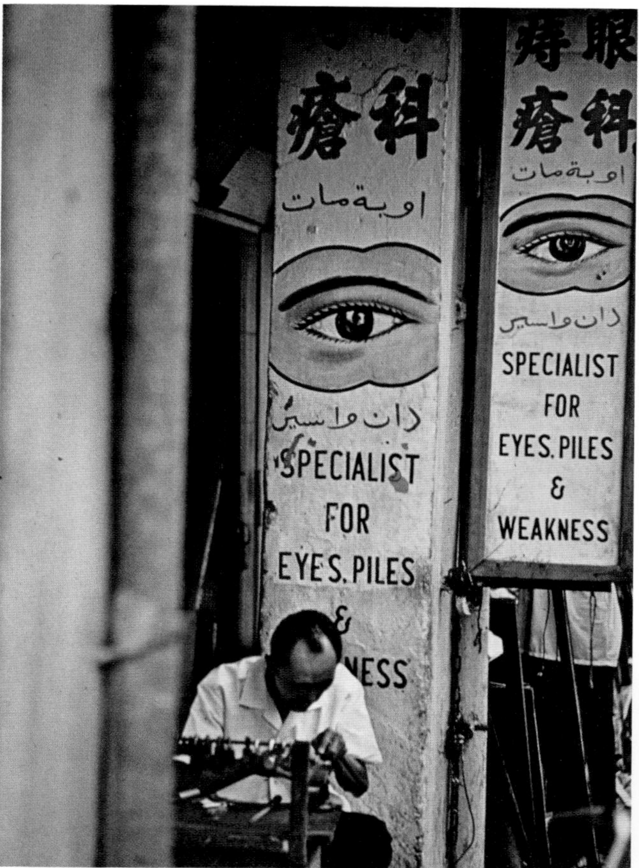

breeze of modern Chinese nationalism wafted down to Singapore towards the end of the 19th century. Dr Sun Yat Sen, founder in 1911 of the first Chinese republic, made trips to see his fellow Chinese – many of them political refugees – scattered over the *Nan-Yang*. He stayed at Singapore. But most of the Chinese there were far too busy and content making money to pay much attention to Sun or to complain of the ills of colonialism. For them the British were protectors. Nevertheless, the first quiet chords of nationalism struck the hearts of quite a few Singaporeans – and this new nationalism was undeniably Chinese – hence today's struggle to stress the multi-racial nature of the nationalism of the present. Chinese Singaporeans began to study Mandarin, the language of Peking and of the Chinese educated élite – although almost all the Chinese of Singapore are descended from southerners.

Nationalism is the Singaporean religion of today. And the dilemma is that although nationalism in Singapore at first meant Chinese nationalism, the government of modern Singapore must strive to give the voice of nationalism a multi-racial ring. Nevertheless, however hard the government may try, Singapore's nationalism carries the trappings and traditions of China. Indians,

A herbalist selling his wares from the street has an equal place beside western trained doctors in Singapore where so many cultures meet.

This Buddhist nun undergoing initiation is one of a declining number. Traditional religion is dying as many Chinese become Catholics.

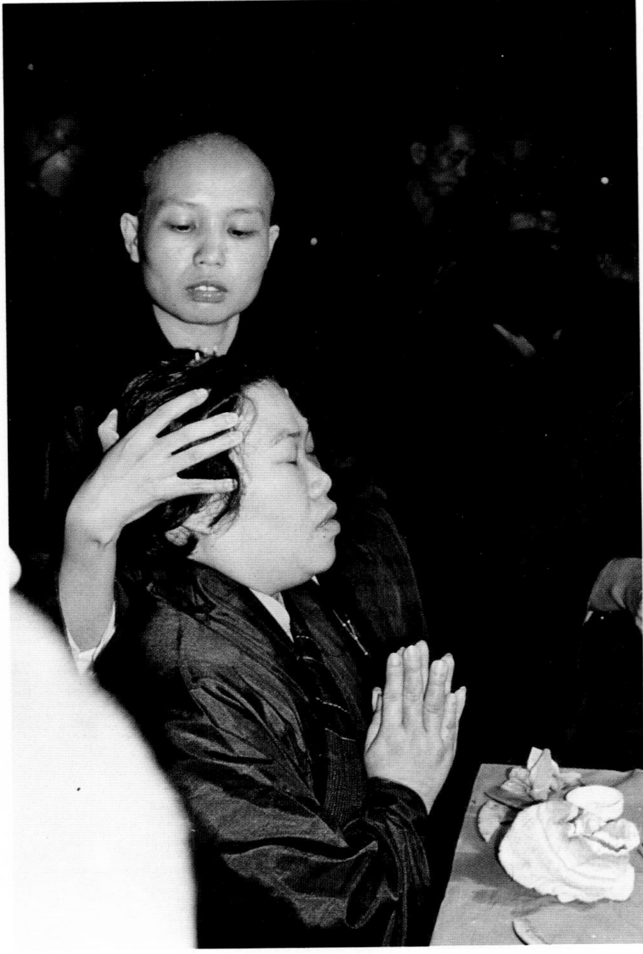

who had their own new brand of nationalism which flowered, then faded, during World War II, when many of them welcomed the Japanese as liberators from colonialism, have come to terms with Singapore's new nationalism and have adapted well. But Malays as a whole have more difficulty, and often feel left out of things, although the government will rightly point to the growing number of Malay officials and politicians in high places. There used to be policies such as 'wet-nursing' whereby a certain number of places were reserved for Malays in the best schools, but these only tended to accentuate the Malay feeling of being second best, and may even have instilled a need to be given special treatment. So those policies have stopped.

Chinese-oriented nationalism is militant and fanatically puritanical. Singaporeans who want to be smart tend to imitate the westerner slavishly, but they do not allow themselves to forget that the west is decadent. The extraordinary enthusiasm that airport officials have for refusing entry permits to male westerners whose hair touches the collar (some of whom would be considered smart, even staid, by western standards) is perhaps unimportant in itself. But it is symptomatic of a regime which in its assertion of independence and cleanliness finds it easy to adopt an aggressively authoritarian pose. In 1971 the pop singer Cliff Richard – mothers' darling, supporter of charities, crusading Christian and opponent of 'permissiveness' – was barred entry because he was adjudged decadent.

The Chinese are accustomed to authoritarian government. By tradition they consider it odd to question the leader. Prime Minister Lee's overwhelming victory at the polls in 1972 – he won every single seat – was claimed by many of the opposition to be rigged, but there is no

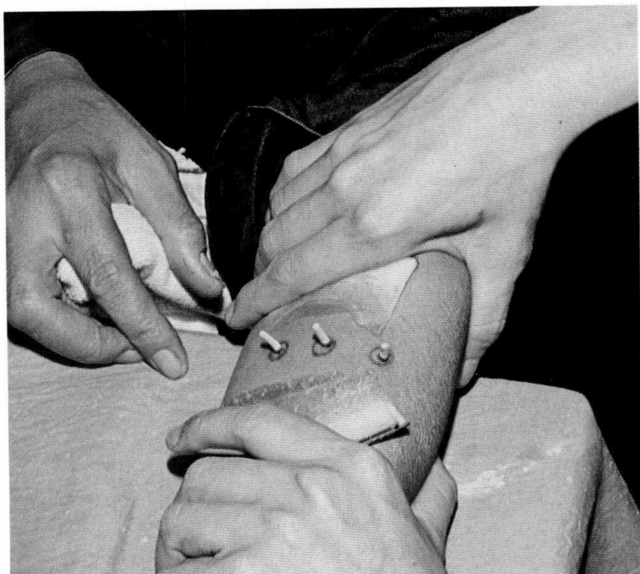

During the initiation ceremony incense cones are placed on the novice's arm and burned to ashes in an offering to Buddha.

Using animals in divination is an ancient practice found in Singapore today where fortune-telling parrots select cards by pecking.

A medium brushes his body with fire in a demonstration of spiritual power. While in a trance mediums are believed to have second sight.

doubt that he has huge and almost total support. The Chinese tend to admire tough leaders. And in their eagerness to be anti-communist (government officials tactfully call their creed 'non-communism') they find it hard to avert their eyes from their natural focal point: Mao's China. Here is another dilemma: few Singaporeans can stifle all praise for mainland China, but they must learn to water it down.

In Singapore worship of the martial arts – which has existed in China for centuries – is keener than ever. Schools for Taikwan-do (unarmed combat) are flourishing. And the most popular films – always so indicative of attitudes – are epics of martial prowess. When they come to avant-garde western cinemas they are invariably censored: the extreme violence, often culminating in swordfights and decapitation, is depicted in relentless detail and with unswerving truthfulness. It would be off the mark to call these films sadistic. They are a brutally frank glorification of physical combat. And of course the good man wins. Revenge is a popular theme, often coupled with the much vaunted virtue of the Chinese: patience. The hero suffers an insult when he is too young to hit back. He takes it coolly, betraying little of his grievance. He nurtures the grudge over the years while he rigorously practises *taikwan-do*. Ten years later he triumphantly repays his oppressor for the insult long since given. Girls rarely feature, but those who do play martial roles as well. Of sex there is but little, and what there is, is highly romanticized. At the end the hero may walk off with the heroine into the dreamy mists, but sex is certainly not revered for itself.

The Chinese of Singapore make less fuss than westerners about sex. In this as in all things they are undemonstrative, although it would be ethnocentric to suggest that they are lacking in passion. A Singaporean told me that the fact that the Chinese do not kiss epitomizes the spiritual, platonic nature of their friendships. Certainly they are more discreet over sex than westerners. Affection between lovers in public would be unusual.

Yet in the early days of Singapore many gang fights broke out over women, largely because the sex ratio was so uneven. In 1881, for example, there were 13 men to every woman. The balance has now been restored, but the homosexuality, inevitable then, is still fairly common today. Bugis Street is famous in the Far East. The government disapproves, but for foreign currency income Bugis Street is good. Taxis drive through it by day, but at night the traffic stops, shopkeepers set up stalls, hawkers shriek their wares, the street is jammed with milling crowds and the heavy hot evening air reverberates with the din of pimps extolling their goods. Groups of American GIs and Australian sailors swagger or stumble along, their confidence buoyed up by their numbers. And the 'Billy Girls' of Bugis Street pick them off one by one. They wear the usual *cheong-sam* (dresses with slits up the sides) and heavy black eye shadow. The surprise

A life-size paper car, to be used by its dead owner in the other world, stands outside a death house before the funeral ritual.

Sent to a death house to die by his family, who believe a death in the home brings evil upon the living, a dead man lies surrounded by offerings.

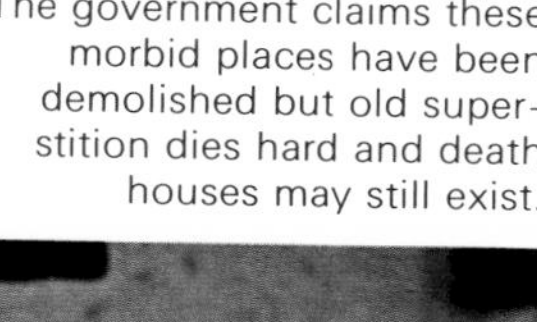

The government claims these morbid places have been demolished but old superstition dies hard and death houses may still exist.

to the ignorant is that the 'Billy Girls' are actually transvestite boys. But Bugis Street is so well known that no heterosexual has ever been known to have 'made a mistake'. For him there are plenty of more conventional whores, who ask the direct question usual in the east: 'Short Time or Long Time?'

But most Singaporeans resent the Sin City image that almost all big ports acquire. After all, it is chiefly the outsider that the pimps are catering for. Most Singaporeans of all races live in tight-knit family circles outside which they rarely venture. The men go off to bars where they drink whisky or brandy. The affluent young go to disco-clubs and dance to western music. Cinemas are generally a male preserve, although the more western the film, the more mixed the audience. The red light area is more for tourists than for Singaporeans. The girls who work there are but a tiny proportion of a huge population. Most girls cherish their virginity before marriage.

In the old days Chinese Singaporeans, if they were rich enough, had one senior wife and several concubines or secondary wives, a system which differed from the Muslim one in that the Chinese wives were not equal to each other. Now Singaporeans are, unless Muslim, officially monogamous. And family planning is forcefully encouraged. A mother gets no maternity leave for having a third child, and loses tax benefits. Families are usually small today, and soon most of them will be living in high-rise blocks. A rise in suicides from the depression often caused by such impersonal and claustrophobic homes is shrugged off by officials: people want modern amenities.

If Singaporean houses have changed, tastes have not. Food is an industry in Singapore, and you can buy food 24 hours of the day. Mothers spend great time and energy cooking Chinese food: rice with meat strongly spiced. If you go out to eat, *sathay* is a favorite: meat roasted on a skewer and dipped in chilis. Brandy and whisky are the most popular drinks.

Gambling is popular as ever, with women losing quite as much money as the men. In bars you often hear the clacking of *mah-jong* tiles together with the click of the chop-sticks. Chinese opera – the *waiyang* – where women are played by men with falsetto voices, apparently improved by a drink of hot water beforehand – is a highly ritualized but ever popular entertainment. There are many fine chess players.

But with the all-pervading stress on cleanliness of mind and body (and of streets, too: you pay a fine of $180 for chucking a cigarette stub out of the window, and Singapore is the cleanest city in Asia) games are the new vogue recreation, especially badminton and swimming. Sport is compulsory at school.

The Chinese of Singapore, leaders of the community but spreaders of the multi-racial gospel, do nothing by halves. Mainly for tourists they continue to hold the traditional festivals and dance traditional dances, but they are energetically westernizing, while equally energetically resisting the 'decadent influences' of the west. Materially there is little of old China left in their customs. But what does remain is perhaps more important: the will to work round the clock, the ruthlessness and vigor to succeed in anything, and the clannishness to keep the secret of success inside the Chinese Singaporean family.

East coast fishermen
Malaya

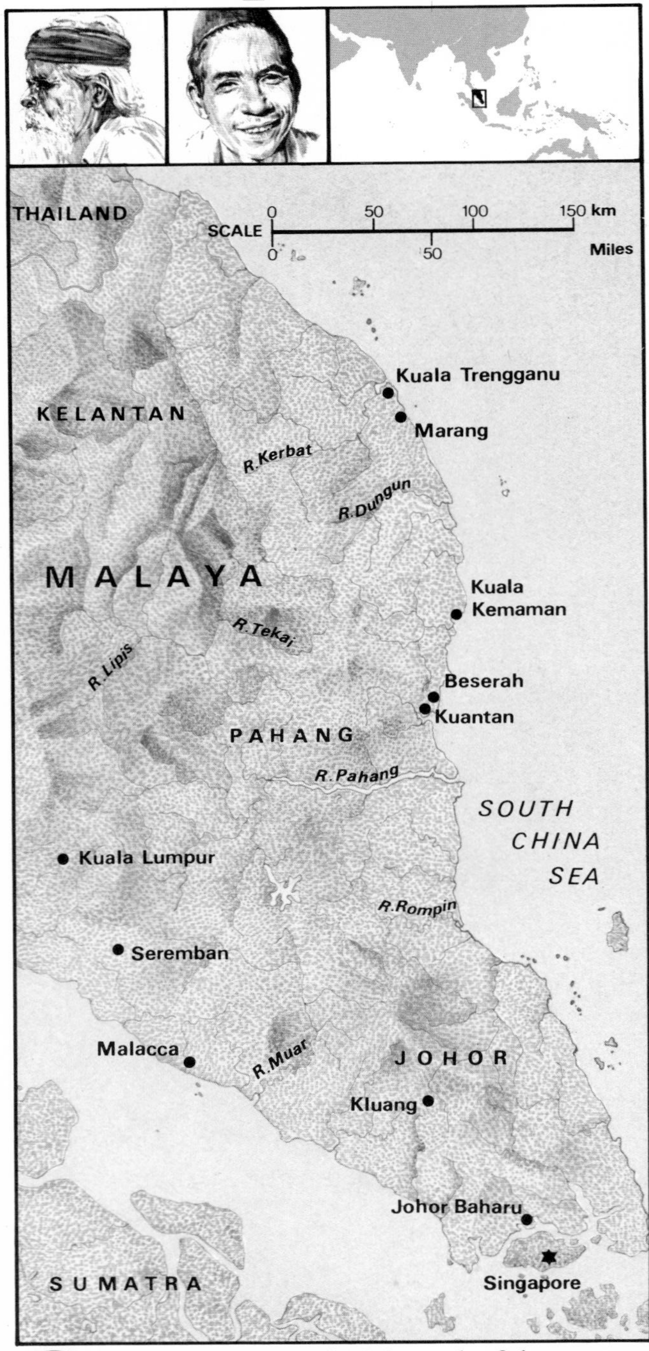

On the north coast of Malaya, the fishermen are called *orang ka laut* which means 'the men who go to sea'. The inland folk, who make their living from the land, mainly by cultivating rice, are called *orang darat*. Throughout most parts of Malaya where rice and fish are the staple foods this distinction between men of the land and men of the sea prevails. The fisherfolk, proud of their skill with boats and nets,

Every group of fishermen on Malaya's east coast has a *juruselam* whose task is to submerge and 'listen' for the shoals of fish.

regard the *orang darat* as mere landlubbers. When they contrast themselves with the rice planters however, they confess that, although they practise a little agriculture, they are not adept at it. The fishermen for example, own neither buffalo nor plows, the symbols of farmers, and only rarely an ox or cow. They are conscious of a calling to their enterprise and may be heard to say 'If I did not fish, how would the *orang darat* get fish? When I die my children too will go to sea, just as when *orang darat* die, their children too will work rice.'

Although the fishermen see themselves as different from the farmers, they see their occupations as complementary and in fact, in coastal areas, the two communities live in close proximity, each carrying out its allotted responsibilities. The small villages or hamlets of rural Malaya are called *kampongs,* a term which includes both the clusters of houses and buildings and also the palm trees, fruit trees and fields which belong to the settlement. In the *kampongs* along the coast each family generally has a small boat with which it can catch enough fish for its needs and also owns a plot of land on which to grow rice. The villagers are often closely related. Most families also have relatives inland on the rice plains and maintain ties with them. They visit each other occasionally, and meet at weddings and other social gatherings.

The fishermen of the east coast use at least a dozen different types of fishing boat. Some own and fish with small one-man boats, traditional boats which are powered by a sail and, when in the shallows, by paddles. All are carvel-built – with the planks flush, and secured by wooden pegs or copper nails – and painted in bright colors. The high, curved prows and sterns sweep down to shallow, undecked hulls. At dawn or in the evening when the boats are drawn up along the beach, between the sea and the towering palms, they make a line – hundreds of yards long – of high prows, pointing skyward.

The different types of boats often have different functions. Some carry the huge seine nets, some the lift nets, and others the mackerel nets. But this specialization is not absolute. In the season of rough weather, the time of the monsoon rains, the larger nets are unsuitable, and then all the boats are used for hand-line fishing.

All these boats, large and small, carry a disproportionate press of sail. The result is that they are unstable in rough weather. A powerful gust of wind can easily heel them over; a heavy sea can quickly swamp them. This is most likely to happen to a boat which has the special job of taking the fish to market, as it races in under too much sail. The boats do not sink altogether; they are usually towed in to shore awash, their catch and their gear all lost. At other times, as the boats approach the beach through a heavy surf, steersmen attempt to ride the breakers and are capsized. Often the catch is lost, although enthusiastic helpers rush out to recover the fish – it is their right to keep or sell them as they wish.

Boats powered by outboard or inboard motors have, over the past thirty years, changed the nature of fishing in east coast Malaya. But the change has been less pronounced than on the west coast. Motors have made larger boats possible, and larger boats carry larger nets, more men and consequently return with a better catch. Sometimes these boats may be at sea for a week at a time; but even the largest are rarely more than 40 or 50 feet long.

Larger boats are often owned by a man who does not participate in the actual fishing. His investment in the boat and its equipment is between 3,500 and 20,000 US dollars. This amount can only be raised by a small number of people – many of whom are Chinese – and often the owner is not even a part of the fishing community and does not live in the *kampong.* The absentee owners employ a local man to captain the boat and to supervise all the administration as well as the fishing.

It is strange that, in this situation of an advancing money economy, fishing in Malaya is still a stronghold of tradition. Boats and other equipment, for example, are never loaned in return for a rent, nor is labor paid for in the form of wages. The old system of sharing the proceeds of a fishing venture is still firmly entrenched. The apportioning of shares, or *bahagian,* has undergone certain changes, but essentially there is still *bahagian* for the boat, the net, and other equipment, the crew, and for the captain or diver. A non-owner captain or diver will receive a larger share than members of the crew. It is not the catch itself which is shared out, but the sales value – after setting aside fish for each crew member to take home for his own family, and deducting the expenses of the trip, such as food and fuel. The cash is shared out at intervals agreed upon by all concerned, not necessarily after each trip.

Between the extremes of one-man boat owners and absentee large boat owners, there are a majority of fishermen who either work for someone else or own a medium sized boat of their own, on which they employ others. This owner may be a *juruselam,* a diver. By tradition the most important man on board, he has a very special expertise, a source of prestige and respect from the crew. He can locate shoals of fish and identify their species just by listening into the water. A good catch tends to be attributed to his skill alone. Fishermen may often leave one boat and join another just to accompany a successful *juruselam.* But today, in the motorized boats, a captain or *jerugan* is more likely to be the owner of the boat, and has largely replaced the *juruselam,* whose role has now been eroded by advances in technology. *Unjangs* (fish playgrounds), for example, have been built from coconut palm fronds, attached at intervals to ropes which stretch from the surface to the sea-bed between wooden floats and weights made of sand-bags.

Every type of fishing, whether in large or small boats, demands skill, hard work and knowledge of local condi-

Fishermen sail before sunrise to catch shoals of Spanish mackerel but with only hand-lines or small nets they are unlikely to catch much.

Children play in the grounds around the cemetery of the mosque at Kuala Kemaman. Like most Malays, they come from devout Muslim families.

At Marang children on their way to school walk through the village past women cleaning fish in stilt huts next to their houses.

East coast fishermen Malaya

The last fishing trip was successful, a fresh catch is carried up the beach at Kuala Kemaman past fish traps stacked to dry in the sun.

Inland Malays and Chinese alike eat pungent dried fish. Without skilled drying the catch would go bad within a few hours.

tions for what is really a small reward, largely determined by chance. Beyond the vagaries of chance the margin between success and failure is small. There may be a small error in the shooting of a net, in the setting of a trap, or in the operation of even a single hand-line. Any of these mistakes can result in an empty-handed return to the *kampong*. Because Malay fishing is a traditional occupation, most ventures are entrusted to the command of a master fisherman, a renowned *juruselam,* or a respected captain. Often his skill and knowledge is bolstered by a reputation for knowing the rituals necessary to propitiate the spirits and attract fish. Associated with this may be certain rituals, such as avoiding mention of the names of certain land animals when at sea.

In the *kampong* too, where people tend to live in a similar style irrespective of the regard in which they are held, the *juruselam* is a respected figure. He has a status second only to that of the village heads, the *ketua kampong* and a standing in the community which goes above the *pawang,* the magician, and the *imam* the prayer leader. None of these men displays a life-style that makes him stand out from the rest of the community. All fishermen in the *kampong* go to the same mosque or prayer house, and frequent the same coffee shops – the two most important social meeting places of the village where the only noticeable social difference is that the richer fishermen occupy the front seats in the mosque while in the coffee shops poorer fishermen and crewmen tend to be more relaxed and vociferous when they are among themselves.

The margin between success and failure for a fisherman is small. Often it depends only on where he sets his fish trap.

Women and other people in the *kampong* who do not go to sea often work at ancillary crafts which supply the fishermen. As the coastal areas yield few of the materials they require, supplies are imported in all stages from the raw material to the manufactured. From the inland districts comes bamboo for fish-curing trays, baskets and net-drying rests; rattan for occasional fish-traps and all kinds of lashings; pandanus leaf sheets for covers; resin with which to caulk the boats; and timber for the boats themselves. From the west coast comes mangrove bark for dyeing nets. In the past China supplied twines and nets. Increasingly nylon and other synthetic materials are being imported from abroad for making nets. The outboard and inboard motors are also imported. This tendency to use imported goods has produced an expanding number of trading middlemen in the same way that dealers have become important to the large-scale fishermen. It has also meant that the fishing communities suffer from price fluctuations in these goods, which bear little relation to the state of the market for their fish.

Fishing in Malaya has come a long way from a purely subsistence occupation. It depends for its prosperity on market conditions. There is a fresh fish market which, with the improvement in transport facilities and roads, and the plentiful supply of ice for storage, has extended from local to inland centers. There is also a market for cooked fish. This allows for a longer handling period, but even so the fish do not keep for many days. The most important market in most areas is for dried or cured fish which may be transported great distances, stored for long periods, and used in times of bad weather or in seasons when fish are scarce. It also provides the means for dealing with a temporary glut.

In recent years, the advances in boat size and equipment, their increasing cost, and the changes in the structure of the market for fish have brought a greater need for specialization. Fishermen are less involved than they were in rice growing and more and more of them now depend entirely on fishing for their livelihood. The catches made by the larger boats are no longer for local sale, but transported inland or to the big towns. Chains of wholesalers and retailers have grown up as the link between the fishermen and the market. At the local level, fishermen deal only with *peraih,* or local dealers who sell the fish at larger markets. Some larger dealers act as agents for wholesalers who supply towns or export dried fish. Other dealers are boat owners as well and also provide the fishermen with nets and other gear. Just as a bond of comradeship exists between divers or captains and their crews, there is also a har-

A fisherman's wife, daughter and grandchildren wait anxiously for his return: boats carrying too much sail are easily swamped or capsized.

(Right) The advent of large motor boats changed the Malay fishing industry, but it is the Chinese who control them and profit the most.

monious relationship between boat-owners and their employees. The owners can be a source of credit in times of hardship; dealers (or absentee owners) may also advance goods like rice and cloth to fishermen against the security of future catches. They often lend money to purchase boats and nets, or sometimes supply the equipment without charge. In return they contract with the fishermen to take the fish at an agreed price, often below the market rate. In this way dealers frequently shoulder a great part of the market risks and help fishermen through thin seasons.

The credit system has the drawback that it places fishermen firmly in debt, with little chance of building up capital of their own. This causes resentment which can easily turn to the kind of anti-Chinese feeling common in many fields of business in Malaya. The Chinese have a reputation for hard-headed business acumen and stand to control a great deal of Malayan commerce. As absentee owners of fishing boats (known as *tauke*) they are gradually moving into a monopoly position, leaving the fishermen with little prospect of reaping the reward of a rising market.

On the east coast it is mainly as middlemen, as dealers or wholesalers, that the Chinese have entered the fish market. The trade in dried and cured fish is predominantly in their hands, possibly because any large-scale export trade requires distant business connections and a supply of capital which will show an immediate return. The extent of Chinese ownership and control of the fishing industry as a whole, however, would be harder to gauge. On the east coast there are some 24,000 fishermen producing about 64,000 tons of fish a year, the majority of whom are Malays, whose boats, even when financed by Chinese, are often registered by Malays. And it is clear that while the larger boats which fish off-shore are likely to be financed or owned by Chinese, the smaller in-shore boats with correspondingly smaller catches are owned and operated by Malays.

With these changes there has inevitably been conflict between the larger boats which do not restrict themselves to off-shore fishing, and the small boats which can only fish in-shore. In-shore fishermen complain that the trawl nets and baskets from the large boats come into their waters and scoop up everything including the baby fish. Small-scale fishermen suffer because of the zeal of the large-scale operators.

Changes in the nature of the Malay fishing industry have foreshadowed many changes in the lives of the fishermen. New conflicts and new antagonisms have developed, some of which are directed at the Chinese who have come to play such an important part in their lives. Larger catches which have accompanied the switch to larger boats, specialization, and motors giving a wider range should have brought greater prosperity – and where prosperity does not appear, the Malays feel themselves deceived.

Peoples of the Philippines

A Filipino creation legend tells of a world which consisted of nothing but sea and sky and only one living creature, a solitary bird. It flew for year after year over the waves finding nowhere to land. At last, tired with flying aimlessly around, the bird provoked an argument between sea and sky and retired to a safe distance to see the outcome. The sea raged, and churned foaming crests of great waves up at the sky, while the sky howled and rolled thunder across the sea. As hostilities increased the sea became even more vehement and the sky began to fling lightning, boulders and great clods of earth at the sea so that gradually a few pieces of land appeared above the waves. After all was quiet the cunning bird flew down to land in the now-created Philippine islands – over 7,000 of them and all erratically shaped.

Scientists also believe that the Philippines had violent beginnings. It is thought that once they and Borneo were one land mass thrown up by volcanic eruptions in the ocean bed, possibly as long as 65 million years ago. Then through a series of eruptions and earthquakes they became split up. On each side of the Philippines are very deep ocean troughs, the South China Sea on the west and the Philippine Trough or Emden Deep on the Pacific side, reputedly the second deepest ocean trough in the world, descending to 34,218 feet within a hundred miles of the shores of Mindanao.

The largest islands of the Philippines are Luzon in the north – which is only about 500 miles from Taiwan – and Mindanao in the south-west, off which is Jolo, only about 150 miles from Borneo. Mindoro, Samar, Panay, Negros and Bohol lie in the central area and the long thin island of Palawan skirts the west. Despite the great number of islands the total land area is only half the size of Arizona or about the same size as Wales.

The history of the Filipinos themselves is as rugged as the history of their land. The earliest known peoples there are the Negritos and the proto-Malays. They survive in some areas, retaining their own cultures to a greater or lesser extent: but, from 300 AD onwards, Chinese, Indonesians, Japanese, Hindus, Spanish and Americans have all contributed their separate influence, creating a diverse population, so that today the term Filipino means little more than does the term American.

The complexity of Filipino society is enhanced by the complexity of the islands themselves. Although lying in the tropical zone the mountains over 5,000 feet high are quite cold and not at all humid. The highest mountains of Luzon and Mindanao are covered with pine forests. Violent typhoons from the western Pacific periodically sweep over the islands causing great destruction.

For thousands of years the Negritos have lived in this setting. The most ancient of all Philippines peoples, they are under five feet in height, with curly hair, dark skin, tinged with yellow, and broad heads. They live deep in the forest, and, being shy, are rarely contacted. They were thought to number less than 15,000 in the 1960s. A typical Negrito group such as the Aeta lives a simple nomadic forest existence wandering in search of game, wild fruit and vegetables and perhaps fishing the mountain streams. Existing groups live in western Luzon, in the lower mountains of eastern Luzon, in the upland interiors of Panay and Negros islands, in the north-east of Mindanao, and in the upland areas of northern Palawan. They are believed to have come from south-east Asia, probably across glacial bridges during the last ice-age.

The proto-Malays who also appear to have come from south-east Asia brought a sedentary way of life, based on rice cultivation. It is difficult to distinguish today the ethnic origins of remote tribes. All one knows is that there are very old, existing, cultures brought in by these peoples at some time or other. No one yet knows the ethnic origins of the now world-famous Tasaday of south-west Mindanao; it is only known that they have a simple culture similar to the Negritos except that they do not hunt animals. These groups of people lived in small numbers and moved about quite a lot because they farmed on a basis of shifting cultivation.

In the southern Philippines only a few such ancient groups survive, threatened as they were by Muslims from the 12th century onwards. In Mindanao are the Manobo, Bagobo, and the Tiruray. The Mangyan live on Mindoro and the Tagbanua on Palawan. In Luzon in the north more and larger groups survived so that today they speak their own languages and retain their own cultures, beliefs and individualities. The Bontoc, the Ifugao, the Kalinga and the Apaugao live like this. The Banawe rice terraces in northern Luzon vividly reveal the antiquity of these peoples' way of life. Built by the Ifugao over 3,000 years ago they are amazing. Each terrace is only from two to eight feet in height, yet together they stretch in a great staircase up 5,000 feet of mountainside. If each terrace was placed end to end they would reach more than half-way round the world.

The Malays who came in were from the western half of the Indies and South-east Asia and were probably Indonesians. They introduced a more mongoloid stock to the islands than was there before. They also brought with them a boat culture and a sea-faring way of life such as that followed by the Bajau Laut in the Sulu islands. Nearly all the peoples of the southern Philippines today are officially regarded as Muslims and the Bajaus are nominally so, but they are regarded by their neighbors as pagans as they retain many of their old beliefs.

By 300 AD the Indonesians were well established along the coastlands. But the three oldest peoples, the Negritos, proto-Malays and Malays were not left in peace for long. Today it is difficult to distinguish the Malays for they have become interbred. All one knows is that there are people in the Philippines who still continue the ways of life of the ancient inhabitants of the country, who are believed to be their forbears.

Chinese accounts written in the 10th and 13th centuries tell of trading voyages to the Philippines and it is fairly certain that then there were Chinese living and trading along the coasts who bought glass beads, porcelain and silk in exchange for sandalwood. Following the ancient Chinese tradition of taking wives from the local populace, they soon added their share to the Filipino racial melting pot. More Indonesians from the great sea-empire of Majapahit in the south filtered into the western island of Palawan and into Sulu and other southern Philippine islands. At this time there were Hindus coming in as well, again as traders. By 500 AD Islam had firmly established itself in the south and by the end of the 16th century the Spaniards were settling Luzon.

By the time Magellan came to the Philippines in 1521 the Filipino people who had come into contact with outsiders had evolved a distinct culture influenced by their many and complex foreign contacts. In the southern islands people communicated in Sanskrit. Their folklore, metal-work, dress and art all showed traces of Hindu life.

They had adopted an alphabet from the Hindus, they wrote with sharp sticks of iron on pieces of bamboo, bark, banana leaves or earthenware. They had a calendar of twelve months in each year, seven days a week and thirty days for each month except the last which had 26. This meant each year had 356 days. They had laws, some written, some unwritten, systems of weights and measures and a society stratified into nobility, freemen and slaves.

When the Spaniards arrived and first brought the Philippines to the notice of the western world, they found a relatively advanced culture. They gave the islands their present name after Philip II of Spain. The Filipinos offered little resistance to the Spanish and in some parts even welcomed them. The Spaniards' biggest struggle was with the Muslims in the southern islands, whom they hated anyway, having tried unsuccessfully to drive their counterparts out of Spain. In fact they never really conquered them at all, and still today the Moros, as the Spanish called them, after the Moors in Spain, have their own ways of life, customs and laws outside the Filipino system. Up until 1837 the Spanish suffered from almost continual piratical raids from the Moros. To the Moros the more Christians they killed the quicker they would get to heaven. One particularly fervent sect used to wrap themselves with bandages all over so that any wounds they might receive would be tourniqueted in advance and they would lose as little blood as possible. This meant they could go on fighting and killing. Eventually in 1851 the Spanish Governor stormed the Moros' stronghold in the southern island of Jolo and put an end to any real power held by the Muslims. From then on they were tolerated as long as they caused no trouble.

Although Magellan discovered the Philippines in 1521, it was not until 1571 that Manila was founded by the Spaniard Legapazi. It was settled by Spaniards from the home country and from Mexico and Peru. It was a Spanish colonial city like any found in the New World. Now this Manila is in ruins, destroyed by a series of earthquakes and heavily bombed in World War II. Its cobbled streets, elegant plazas and tile-roofed houses have all fallen into decay. The oldest building in the Philippines is the San Augustin Church, first built of nipah palm and bamboo and later rebuilt of stone and adobe and completed in 1601. San Tomas University still stands, founded in 1605 originally for young Spaniards entering the church.

Although the Filipinos first treated the Spanish with hospitality they soon hated them for their arrogance. The Spanish established a feudal system in Manila in which the Filipinos had to do all the hard labor. The Chinese traders hated the Spanish too, for the restrictions they placed on their trading enterprises. But the Spanish exploitation could have been worse. They found no lucrative deposits of gold or other precious minerals and they discovered none of the spices which were so valuable in the 16th century. But the land laws and the arrogant attitude of the friars led to a final revolt in 1897 with dreadful atrocities on both sides. In the next year the Philippines passed to the United States.

During the first half of the 19th century there were only 2,000 to 5,000 Spaniards in the Philippines. A lot of troops came in to quell the uprisings but when the Spanish went out still only very few Filipinos could speak Spanish. The most notable legacy left by the Spanish was their religion. Today the Philippines is the only Asian country that is predominantly Catholic.

As soon as the Americans moved in they immediately began to teach English in the schools and very soon English became the most widely understood language. It still is today although Tagalog, the native language of the central lowlands of Luzon, is the national language and is now also taught in schools. The Philippines have enormous potential. They grow great quantities of rice and corn, and fruit, nuts and root crops, beans and peas, coffee, cacao and peanuts. They have a lot of forest wealth especially in hardwoods. Fishing plays an important part in the economy and so does mining of gold, silver, iron, copper, chrome, manganese and lead. They have a varied industrial economy. They have food processing factories, oil refineries and chemical factories.

Today Manila looks something like Chicago with its tower blocks of steel, concrete and local marble. Its noisy streets, blaring horns, and numerous crimes and murders remind one of an American gangster city.

The saddest aspect of Filipino society is that its politics are so openly corrupt. Political killings are commonplace as is crime of all kinds. Filipino society is a long way from having learned to live with, and in, its teeming cities.

Tasaday
Mindanao

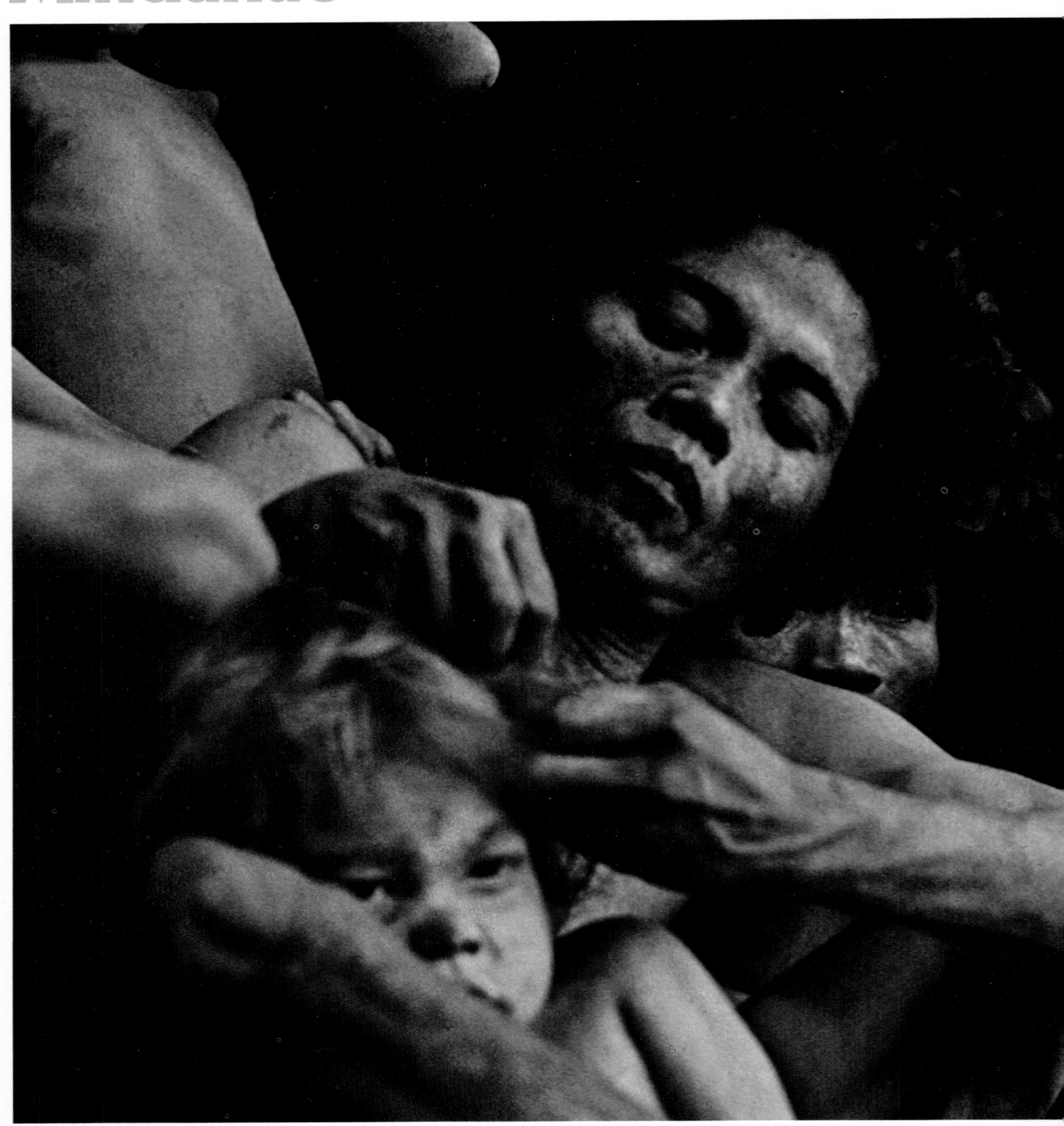

There are only 24 Tasaday; a 20th century stone age tribe of gentle, contented people isolated in mountainous jungle for over 600 years.

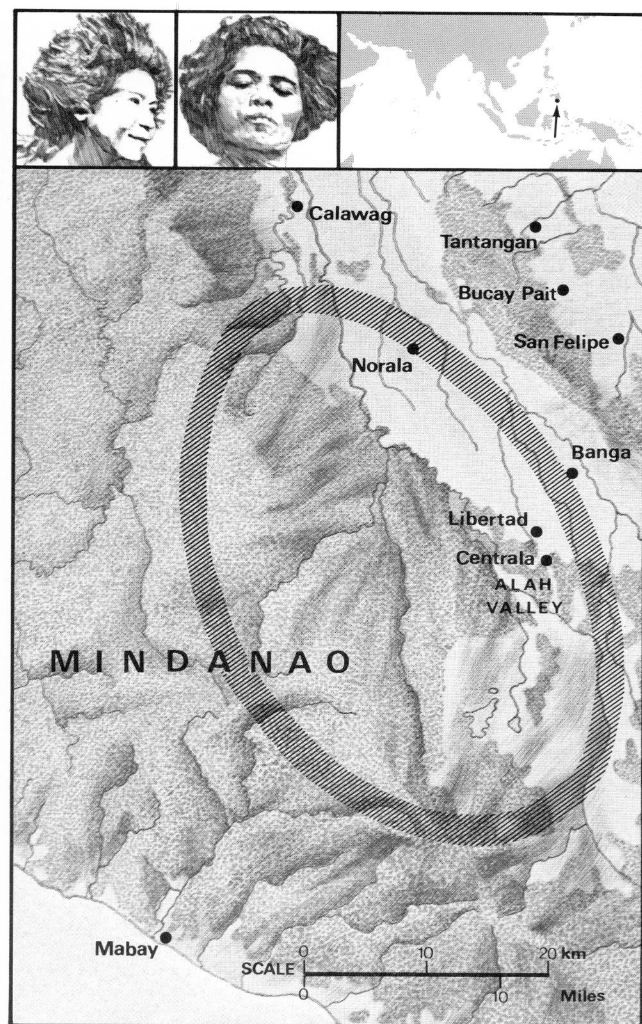

The world heard of the Tasaday for the first time in mid-1971. 'Stone Age People discovered in the Philippines,' 'Tasadays meet the world' ran the newspaper headlines. Within a few months the brief initial reports were followed by color photographs in magazines and film on television. The Tasaday were news! Yet despite this apparent subjection to the media, only a little solid information has been released up to the time of writing.

As the anthropologist who works in the field must learn the Tasaday language and live with them for a year or more before he can make a thorough study, and even then will need time to write up his data and publish it, one is tempted to ask why the publicity at this stage? Wouldn't it have been better to keep the discovery from the world's press until the study was complete? Or even just to have left the Tasaday alone in their jungle world? The answers lie in the more general situation of minority tribal peoples in the Philippines and indeed in the whole

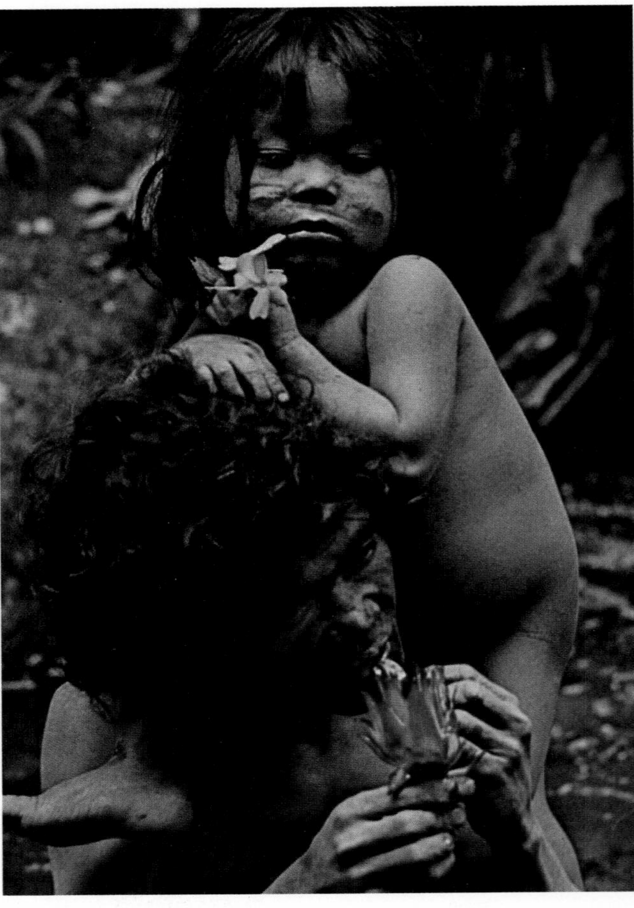
The Tasaday have no need to kill animals; the jungle provides all the food they want, and collecting it takes only a few hours a day.

world.

The Tasaday are a small tribe who live in the Cotabato Cordillera (Tiruray Highlands) of south-western Mindanao. Their home is about fifteen miles from the mountain Dataltabayung near Lake Sebu in the central part of the Cordillera. The highlands stretch for some 125 miles from north-west to south-east along the Celebes Sea coast of south-west Cotabato province, and are about 35 miles across between the sea and the interior lowlands of the Cotabato and Allah valleys. Although the mountains reach over six thousand feet in the south, they average only three or four thousand feet. Nor are they especially rugged, but travel in them is made difficult by the dense jungle of tropical evergreen forest. Until recently the mountains remained inaccessible, for few roads approached them, and much of the interior remained only partly explored. This remoteness has made the hills the last stronghold or refuge of the pagan tribes of Cotabato.

These hill peoples are few in number and very scattered. They are not organized in large political groups, and their villages are small. They divide culturally into three main groups speaking three distinct mutually unintelligible but structurally similar languages: the Tiruray in the north, the Manubo (Manobo) further south, and southernmost of all the T'boli or Tagabili. These languages have an original common stock within the Malayo-Polynesian language family. Until after World War II when the government began sponsoring settlement schemes in their province and Christian settlers came flooding in the hill peoples remained in isolation. The population density of Cotabato in 1903 was 14 per square mile: by 1960 it had jumped to 130. The diverse origins of the surrounding and impinging population, who also included Moros (Muslims), Maguindanao and Sangil have led to serious clashes on many issues, particularly landownership, the economy and politics. In the conflicts the Moros have tended to favor violent direct action; the Christians, the courts. Before this onslaught the indigenous groups have simply wilted. Some have been converted and assimilated. Others, clinging to their own cultures, have been forced from their traditional territories deeper and deeper into the hills. Uneducated, they have been unable to fight their battles against land-grabbers and timber concessionaires in the courts. Unorganized and poorly armed, they have been unable to meet force with force.

Over time a number of champions have appeared to defend the hill peoples' rights. Realizing that it was futile to attempt to stem the flood of settlement, they have concentrated on trying to mitigate the effects of change on these vulnerable people with legal protection, education and medical help. Early in 1971 one of their champions Manuel Elizalde, Junior, the Presidential Assistant on National Minorities and founder of the Private Association for National Minorities (PANAMIN) was

An impenetrable barrier of jungle kept outsiders away for over 600 years, but Tasaday know how to move swiftly through their dense forest.

Tadpoles, frogs and crabs, easily caught by agile hands from jungle streams are wrapped in palm leaves and roasted.

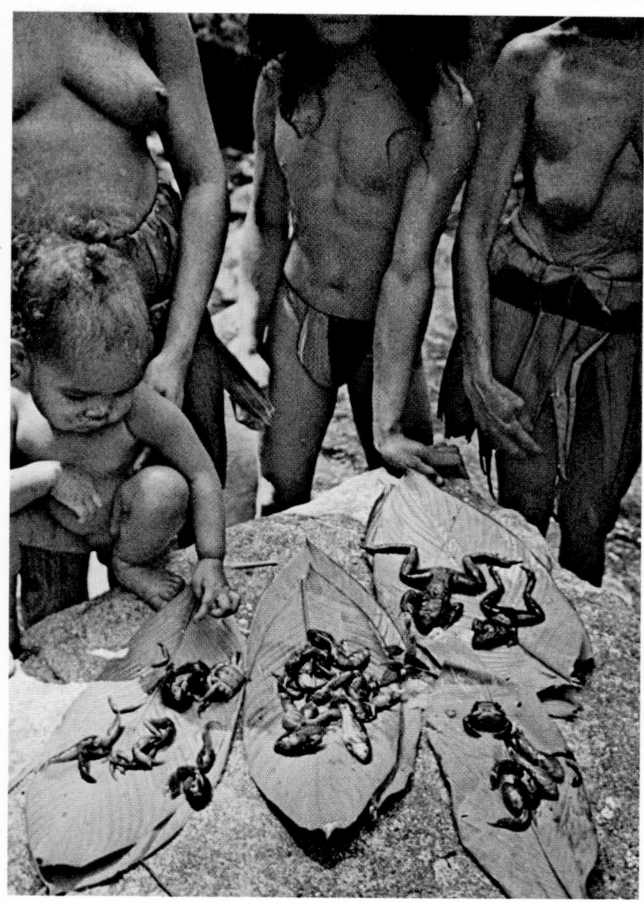

(Over page) Anthropologists believe the Tasaday are the only men ever discovered in modern times who make their permanent homes in caves.

Dafal the hunter taught the Tasaday how to make *natek* from the pith of a large palm. Roasted cakes of *natek* are now their favorite food.

working among the Ubo when one, an Ubo hunter named Dafal, told him of a tribe in the interior hills who were hitherto completely unknown. These were the Tasaday.

Dafal insisted that this strange tribe used only stone tools. They subsisted, he said, only by gathering the products of the forest and had no weapons. In the context of the Cotabato hills this was startling information. For all the hill peoples are farmers even if they are only relatively unsophisticated slash-and-burn shifting cultivators. All use steel tools and carry weapons. Elizalde brought in Dr Robert Fox, the doyen of Philippine anthropology. Fox and Elizalde made a number of visits to them to find out such basic anthropological facts about them as their language, their material culture, their kinship relations, their history and their religious beliefs. Language problems made all this very difficult. Although Tasaday turned out to be related to Manubo-Blit (both appear to be descended from an ancestral language), their relationship is distant. For example Inga, a Manubo-Blit woman who helped with the translation from Tasaday into T'Boli (which could then be translated directly into English), initially understood about 50 per cent of the Tasaday language, and Dafal only one word in five. Once the official preliminary investigations had been completed, Fox and Elizalde decided to announce the Tasaday's existence to the world. In March 1972 Elizalde escorted a selected party of anthropologists, newsmen and photographers into the jungle by helicopter to meet the Tasaday. This was a crucial decision, but the Tasaday had already met the modern world, for they had met Dafal. And in five years he alone had produced some striking changes in their material culture. The problem was not how to preserve the Tasaday's simple culture, for that was impossible anyway, but how to ensure that the Tasaday should have some control over their own destiny. The problem was ultimately how to protect them from being crushed, or worse, by the encroaching outside world. President Marcos responded rapidly to the crisis and set aside 46,299 acres as a reserve for the Tasaday and their close neighbors the Manubo-Blit in 1972. This effectively constituted recognition of tribal land rights and was a very important step for Elizalde as it gave him the necessary legal backing with which to organize the Tasaday's protection *before* they were exposed to attack. Three logging roads had already begun to penetrate the forests surrounding the reserve.

On further acquaintance the Tasaday turned out to be a tiny tribe. When discovered in June 1971 they were just 24 in number; ten adult men, five adult women and nine children, most of them boys. Asked if there were any other people like them in the forest they said there were two other groups, the Sanduka and the Tasafang, although they had not seen them for some time. One of the Tasaday women was in fact a Sanduka, married to a Tasaday man. They are physically well built, but quite short. The men are a little under five feet tall with medium

Three men take it in turn to rotate a stick in a notched log until tinder can be lit from the friction heat of the notch.

(Center) The Tasaday were only discovered in 1971 but already they prefer to use lighters instead of the laborious drilling stick.

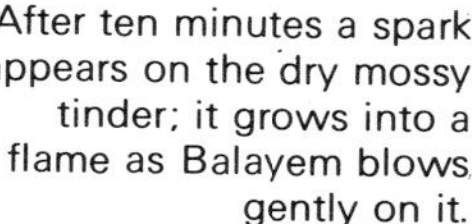

After ten minutes a spark appears on the dry mossy tinder; it grows into a flame as Balayem blows gently on it.

Two fires are kept alight in the cave all the time, for cooking during the day and for warmth at night when the rain forest grows cold.

brown skin, black eyes, wavy black hair, and look entirely beardless, as they pluck out their sparse growth of hair on the chin. Apart from a few goitres they seem healthy. Goitre is common elsewhere in the Cotabato hills, among the Manubo for example, and is associated with iodine deficiency in the diet. The Tasaday diet is entirely salt-free, which may explain the lack of iodine.

Their dress is simplicity itself. Both men and women wear a pouch over the genitals made from orchid palm leaves. Over this the women wear a leaf skirt. Men wear wooden earplugs through pierced earlobes. The women wore no ornaments until Dafal sold them bead necklaces and bronze earrings.

They live in some caves in the side of a cliff surrounded by dense forest. The largest of their caves has an entrance about fifteen feet high and about twice that width, and goes back some fifty feet into the cliff. In the cave they keep two fires constantly burning, partly for cooking and partly to keep themselves warm. The forest can become quite cool at night and the Tasaday sleep on the ground without any bedding. If they sit it is on any convenient piece of wood or stone, but in fact they usually squat on their haunches. The furnishing of their caves is completed by large bamboo segments which they use to carry water up from the stream and to store it in. When they need to make a fire they usually light it from existing fires, but the Tasaday method of making fresh fire is with the fire drill. They put the end of a stick into a notched log, and then rotate it between the palms of their hands until tinder can be ignited from the friction heat within the notch.

Until the late 1960s, their economy was strictly based on gathering forest produce. It remains largely unaltered. Over a territory of about two-and-a-half miles in radius they collect a wide variety of forest products: wild bananas, wild ginger and rattan fruits, palm cabbage and other fruits, nuts, berries and leaves which are as yet unidentified. They eat certain flowers and fruits raw on the spot, and bring back other items to the cave to be cooked. With digging sticks they pull up roots, particularly the wild yam (*biking*), which was once their staple food. From streams they take small fish, frogs, tadpoles and crabs, wrap them in leaves and roast them. Fat grubs from rotten logs are something of a delicacy. They chew betel (areca nut), which stains their mouths bright red.

Their technology matches their economy. They use split bamboo to provide a sharp knife-edge, and stone scrapers to trim wood, thus sharpening their digging sticks, for example. Their most elaborate, most handy, and most useful tool is the stone axe – a largish split pebble, rubbed down on rock to a rough edge, inserted into a cleft stick handle and held in place with rattan strip. It can be used as an axe to split firewood or chop open soft or rotten tree trunks in the search for food. Or it becomes a hammer for breaking fruit shells, crushing areca nuts or cracking bamboo. Or again it is a scraper for sharpening the digging sticks or shredding bark for timber. It is not, however, sharp enough to deal with hard woods, and it was not considered as a weapon, for they were not hunters and had no foes to fight.

The arrival of Dafal the Ubo hunter in 1966 changed the Tasaday's dependence on this simple economy and technology. He taught them how to trap and kill animals such as the deer, pigs and monkeys. Although the Tasaday had suspected that meat would be good food, they had felt it was unnecessary to eat it as they had never been hungry on their previous diet. And they were reluctant to lose their previous close relationship to animals. The Tasaday said that unmolested, the animals had been their friends. However, in exchange for meat, which he taught them how to preserve by smoking, Dafal gave them a bow and arrow and a spear, for which they had no use, some cloth which proved popular for warmth and a *bolo*, a local kind of jungle knife with a long heavy steel blade set in a wooden handle. For the Tasaday this was a revolutionary new technology, for with it they could exploit a whole new range of food sources. Of these the most important is *natek*, the pith of a large palm tree. Dafal had to instruct the Tasaday in some complex techniques to extract and prepare it. The pith has to be pounded to shreds with bamboo pounders, poured with water through a filter of leaves, down a gutter into a settling trough. The end-product is a starch which is dried and made into small cakes and cooked in the fire. It is now the Tasaday's favorite food.

Little is known yet about Tasaday society, which is based on the elementary family of husband, wife and children. Although there is a high proportion of men to women, the Tasaday are monogamous and marry for life. All the women are married, and men without wives have either to wait until the children grow up, remain bachelors, or try to make contact and find a wife from one of the other forest peoples they claim exist. Only husband and wife are present at childbirth. With a razor-sharp bamboo sliver the husband cuts the umbilical cord and buries it. When the next child is born the first is probably weaned – as a child of three was reported as still suckling. Children are brought up by both husband and wife together. The parents do not use physical punishment but do occasionally rebuke their children.

Everyone in the community shares the available food. If there is a shortage, the children are fed first. There appear to be no divisions of labor, and such differences in tasks as do occur are based on the interests and abilities of the individual. The Tasaday make decisions on a communal basis and have no formal leader. One man did however come forward to act as spokesman for the group to their visitors, and persuaded the Tasaday to come out of the forest for their original meeting with Elizalde.

The Tasaday say that when a person dies his body is taken out of the cave and hidden in the jungle. Should he die in the forest his body is covered up with leaves and

Men wear only a pouch of orchid leaves to protect themselves from thorns and leeches; women wear the same under an orchid palm skirt.

left there. In south-east Asia belief in a soul is fairly widespread; indeed some peoples in this area believe that a person has more than one spirit element in his total makeup. When a person dreams the soul is usually thought to leave the body and wander about, thus creating the experiences of the dream. Sickness is interpreted as a manifestation of the wandering spirit under attack. Death is seen as the soul's departure from the body. It is difficult to be sure what the Tasaday's beliefs are in our present state of knowledge. They have been questioned about them, but it is precisely on topics of this kind that the difficulties of translation become most obvious. They say that they do not know if they have souls. They say they have dreams but do not know what these mean. It is not even clear if they believe in the existence of spirits. Although they prefer to stay in the cave at night this may only be due to fear of practical dangers in the forest, particularly thorns and snakes underfoot. In the daytime they fear thunderstoms, but only apparently for the noise they make and the danger of falling branches.

The Tasaday are even less helpful about their origins. They do not know anything of the wide area around them, and have no word for sea, even though it is so close

(Bottom) Pith from the core of palm trees is beaten to a pulp with bamboo flails. This is poured with water through a leaf filter to make *natek*.

Men make primitive stone tools by splitting pebbles which they rub against other stones to make a sharp cutting edge.

The sharpened stone is inserted into a cleft stick handle and tied in place with strips of rattan.

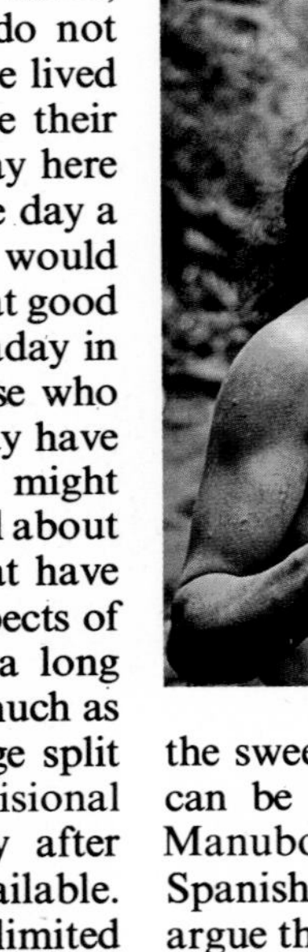

(Bottom) The stone axe is used to cut firewood, crack nuts, and sharpen digging sticks, but it is not a weapon, for the Tasaday have no enemies.

to them. They say they have always lived in their caves, that their ancestors came here long ago. They do not know of any other place in which they might have lived before. They believe that they should never leave their home, as an ancestor dreamt that should they stay here they would not only be safe from disease, but one day a great one – whether man or god is not yet clear – would come to visit them. He would be the bringer of great good fortune. Manuel Elizalde is now cast by the Tasaday in this role, and it is difficult to think of anyone else who might be more capable of filling it. As the Tasaday have no history, and at present lack any myths that might yield clues will it be possible to know anything at all about their origins? Careful analysis of the changes that have taken place in their language offers the best prospects of revelation and linguists are already suggesting a long time-span – at least six hundred and possibly as much as two thousand years – since the Tasaday language split from its ancestral Manubo stock. Good provisional answers may be possible fairly soon but only after prolonged research will detailed knowledge be available. Physical information about the Tasaday type is limited to photographs, but when they can be blood-grouped and thoroughly examined we will certainly learn more about their origins. For the present one can only anticipate that it will be found that the Tasaday are of the general stock of the peoples of the Philippines.

Their material culture is so limited that there is little positive evidence to help make correlations with other peoples. Even music, so often helpful in these matters, is not available. The only known musical instrument associated with them is the *kubing*, a bamboo jew's harp – and this was a gift from the ubiquitous Dafal. Indeed most evidence about their lives tends to be negative. They are, for example, *not* cultivators and have no knowledge of agriculture. Given rice to eat they tried to consume it raw. Nor do they know any other important cereals of the area, such as maize. And they are not familiar with the sweet potato (*camote*) or with tobacco. From this it can be argued that the Tasaday split off from other Manubo-speakers before these crops arrived with the Spanish settlers in the 16th century. One could further argue that their split was probably many centuries earlier as they have no cultivation at all. This argument is not on its own very convincing as collecting groups can live close to farmers for centuries without adopting their economy or food habits. And it is not difficult to conceive that after a few generations of isolation in a fairly abundant environment the Tasaday might completely forget an earlier experience of the agricultural world.

The argument becomes more telling when it is combined with the absence of iron in that culture. Iron tools are so vastly superior to stone or wood tools that it is hard to believe that any people who ever knew iron could subsequently forget it. Now though it is thought that iron came from Borneo to the Philippines after the islands were settled, the Tasaday are the first group of people ever to have been found there without knowledge of it, or indeed any other metal. Their simple split pebble stone

To avoid a six-day trek through the jungle, the Tasaday's visitors arrived by helicopter, 'the big bird with the yellow belly'.

The government has set aside 50,000 acres as a reserve; only just in time, for loggers and miners are eager to exploit the jungle's wealth.

tools, on the other hand, are what we might expect in the forest environment of the Philippines, and confirm archaeologists' findings on the pre-Iron Age of the archipelago. This would suggest a very long period of isolation indeed.

Further evidence is provided by the Tasaday's fire-drill. This method of firemaking, although efficient in a forest area, is primitive and unusual for the Philippines. Prior to the introduction of matches, flint and steel was the most widespread method of firemaking. They have further, no pottery, which is very unusual in the Philippines where for centuries a wide variety of pottery forms have been made and traded. Chinese ceramic wares had been imported and were well-known even among the less sophisticated societies in the Philippines before the Spanish conquest. Instead of pottery, the Tasaday use bamboo sections for carrying and storing water – a common enough device among many hill peoples of south-east Asia. But the only other use they appeared to have for bamboo prior to Dafal's arrival was for knives. This too, is startling in the Philippines where the uses of bamboo are myriad and where it would not be inapt to describe the indigenous peoples as traditionally possessing a bamboo culture. Finally they have no cloth or weaving in a country where *abaca* (Manila hemp) is native and where for considerable time cotton has been in widespread use. If we add all this up it is clear that the Tasaday are either a people who have been isolated for a very long period indeed, or that they are an elaborate hoax. On the available sober evidence, the latter is impossible to believe and must be discounted. The Tasaday are clearly the modern representatives of men from the Philippine stone age.

It is surprising that their culture should be so very limited, particularly in its use of bamboo. It is difficult to attribute this poverty of equipment to anything other than the ability of a small group of people to live off the forest throughout the year without having to recourse to hunting, fishing, cultivating or even storage to ensure their food supply. Since they lack nothing, they do not need to put their efforts into technological invention. Having no contact with other groups and no property or territory to defend, they are entirely pacific. What they do with their leisure time we do not know, although they have possibly a developed poetry, folklore or myth, or a secret religious art not yet shown to the outsiders. But this apparently idyllic situation, where man easily acquires all he needs from the jungle and has abundant leisure time, is marred by the acute shortage of women – which is one of the major factors in keeping the population in its present balance with its environment.

The idyll anyway is now over. The anthropologist, recognizing the force of change, must rapidly complete his records of this one brief glimpse of a stone-age collecting and gathering culture. The Tasaday, having met the world, have to go on and face it.

Moros
Philippines

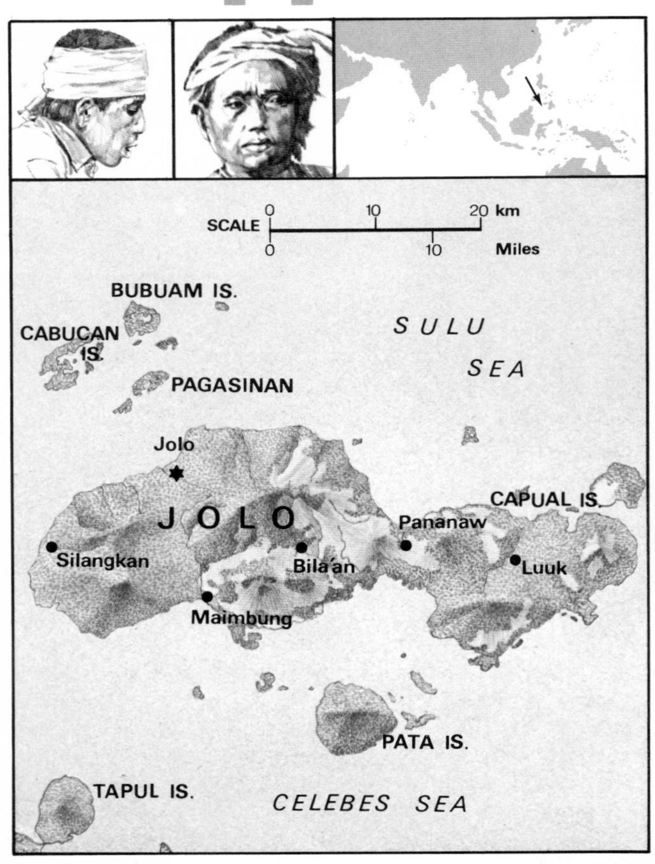

The Philippine Islands are often called the least oriental country in the orient. Most people are Christians, speak English and wear western clothes in a more or less American atmosphere. This is due to Spanish and later to American interference. But there is one group of people who have proudly refused, ever since the Spanish arrived in the 16th century, to adapt their way of life to these new customs. These people are the Muslims of the Philippines, or as the Spanish colonists called them, the Moros. They live quite differently from other Filipinos: even their laws are different, and the Philippines government has been obliged to make legal and other exceptions for the Muslims.

The Muslims' feeling of difference goes back a long way. In the 15th century, long before the Spanish arrivals, Muslim missionaries started to arrive from the south-west, traveling among the scattered Philippines, and trying to convert the Indonesian populations to Islam. By 1500 Islam had a strong foothold in the Sulu archipelago, and had spread to the large island of Mindanao; by 1565 Muslims had got as far north as Manila Bay. When the Spanish arrived in the mid-16th century, Mecca and Rome clashed. There was bitter fighting. Most Filipinos accepted Spanish rule, but the Muslims resolutely refused: this was the beginning of

Fiercely independent, the Moros ('Moors' as the Spanish called them) have clung to their devotion to Islam. Young girls study the Koran in Arabic.

Moro separatism, which has hardly relaxed at all today. Now the 1·5 million Muslims are concentrated on southern islands – on western Mindanao, on Palawan and on the Sulu archipelago.

The Muslims do not look very different from other Filipinos, although their aquiline noses reveal a blending of Arab with Malay blood. Their skin is smooth, dark and sea-tanned. The so-called Moro stare can be very disconcerting. Strangers meet it everywhere, in villages, markets and on fishing wharves. Impassive faces with fixed unblinking eyes boldly inspect strangers. Sometimes the stare changes into derisive, contemptuous-sounding laughter or into shyness. In some places, especially in the Cotobato area on Mindanao, where the Moros chew betel, their expressions are altered by the brilliance of their lips and the redness of their teeth: sometimes their teeth are filed to points, and their eyebrows shaven. Many Moro areas, especially the southernmost islands, are bandit country, remote and lawless, and it can be frightening to go there as a stranger.

The Moros wear bright, usually traditional clothes, although the younger people are beginning to wear western clothes. Men wear sarongs and loose-cut shirts of batik. They also wear the fez, or elaborately twisted turbans, and braided vests which they wear with wide cummerbunds. In these they carry long daggers or perhaps brass boxes containing betel nuts. Women wear tight silk or cotton trousers, tight-sleeved jackets of beautiful lamé and brocade, or bright silk lengths of cloth rather like saris. They often have gold thread running through their silks, and buttons of gold coins. Some have very long polished nails and ankle bells, and perhaps rouge one lip. Both men and women have a long, slow, arrogant stride, and proud bearing. Their grace is memorable.

Muslim clothes and beliefs are particularly vividly displayed at weddings. At a poor fishing village, say on the island of Basilan, among thatched stilt houses over a tidal estuary, between palm trees and a mosque, a typical Muslim wedding would be splendidly celebrated, in a community which survives by fishing and gains what wealth it has from the widespread art of smuggling. Near the bride's house, a four piece orchestra on a canopied platform would play softly. A girl would sing Muslim love ballads, and another might play a *gambong* (a kind of xylophone common throughout Indonesian islands). The bride, wearing her most beautiful clothes and all her gold ornaments, is led to the ceremony and married according to Muslim rites. Chastity is important to the Moros partly because bride prices are high, and adulterous women are punished. The laws of marriage are Muslim and not those of the Philippine government by which divorce and polygamy are illegal. By the Moros' own laws, which the government tolerates, a man may have several wives and repudiate any of them at will. After the wedding ceremony there is always dancing – Moro dances are famous for their beauty. In the *pangalay* three girls in gorgeous sarongs do a gracious courtship dance, and compete for one man's affection. Most impressively dressed are the fierce Yakkan people from the rough jungle country of Basilan. They look like toreadors, in multi-colored jackets and skin-tight trousers, which they cannot take off until they rot from years of use, with massive lengths of striped cloth wrapped round and round their stomachs. These are effectively both blankets and protection against knives. The Yakkans, unlike most Moros who are fishermen and small holders, have a centuries-old reputation for horsemanship. They are related to the Borneo Dayaks.

The Moros fall into four main groups all following caste laws and living in hierarchical groups under *datus* who administer the *agama* courts. The Maranos settled centuries ago on the north-west coast of Mindanao and became farmers and herders in the rich grasslands round Lake Lanao. Here today live some of the richest Moros, and it is here that separatist education for Muslims has developed: it has always been separate, but now the separatism is conscious and organized. They have created the Muslim university of Mindanao in Marawi City, the provincial capital, and rich landowners and others arrange for students to go to Muslim universities abroad. Here too industry is developing, using local hydro-electrical resources. The Maguindos, on the other hand, live along the broad valleys of the Rio Grande de Cotabato where they grow rice in paddy fields. The other two groups are the island people of the Sulu archipelago, the Tausugs and the Samals.

Two-thirds of the Sulu people are Tausug speaking. The Samals are of a different ethnic background and became Muslims later than the Tausugs. The inhabitants of Tawi Tawi, and the famous Orang Laut sea gypsies speak Bajau. The home of all these peoples is a collection of rocky and marshy volcanic islands, set on coral reefs, joined together at low tide and sometimes swept by typhoons. A third of the land is covered in forest or swamp, and there are no minerals, so industry and farming are limited. The islanders get their living from the sea.

Like some Pacific islanders these people can tell their way on the sea from the stars. In fact the people of Tawi Tawi found their reckonings seriously disrupted by the appearance of moving space-craft in the sky: they could not believe that these new, erratic, stars had been cast up there by man, and were therefore irrelevant to their nautical map. They build outriggers or *vintas* hollowed out of tree trunks by adzes, buoyed by twin outriggers, and with a single sail. They go out in bright fleets of 40 or more of these vessels traveling fast and far. During World War II some escaping Samals and Americans sailed 3,000 miles to Australia in an outrigger.

One group of people is so close to the sea, that they only leave the water during bad weather. Huddled into harbors their presence prophesies storms and the mon-

Moros proudly remain isolated; they have their own laws and resist modern American influence as they resisted 16th century Spaniards.

soon. These are the Bajau Laut, sea gypsies (see page 54) some of whom hardly ever land except to sell fish. They have had to become hardy. When a baby is born its father drops it straight into the sea. If it swims it lives. If not it is left to drown.

Other fishing people are more land-bound, and most of them to one place. Some people have small market gardens, or do casual labor, and some have farms of up to six acres. They cultivate coconut, cassava and abaca, and women in wide bamboo hats work for hours among the rice plants in their paddy fields. But the farming in these parts is usually small-scale. Bananas and mangroves grow naturally, with squashes, tropical fruits and betel. Traditional handicrafts are of greater significance here than anywhere else in the Philippines, except among the Maranao Moors of Lake Lanao, and are very highly developed. Now not only do they build their own very swift watercraft, but they make tools in iron and bronze, and work brass, bronze, copper, silver and gold, both for implements and for art, and they make very bright textiles, which stand out against the horizon as the sails of their fishing boats.

The Sulu islanders used to sell button shell of mother of pearl and coral, and shark fin, birds' nests and turtle eggs. But the development of world plastics and synthetics industries, and the closing of the market in mainland China has undermined this industry.

The young groom is carried in procession from his parents' house to the house of his bride, where they will be married.

A miniature bamboo house full of food is a part of the bride price given by the groom's family to the family of the bride.

Bajau Laut
Philippines

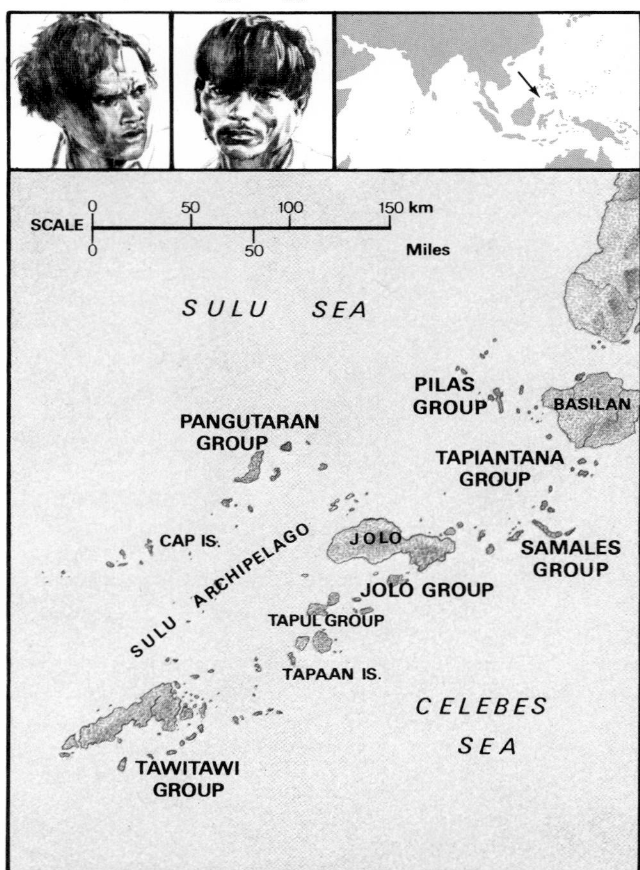

Around the Sulu islands – strung out between the Philippines and northern Borneo – the sea is shallow and teeming with life. Submerged terraces and ledges on this underwater plateau harbor an abundance of sea creatures, seeking the shelter of a lee shore, protection from winds and currents. Above, along the coastline, coral reefs break the force of heavy seas, and in the peaceful estuaries and calm lagoons the Bajau Laut (Bajau *of the sea*) find safe mooring for their boats, and build their villages on stilts out over the water.

The Bajau Laut live by the sea and upon the sea and with the sea and have little to do with the land. Fishing is their way of life, for the women and children as much as for the men. Each family has its boat – which is often a home as well – and from birth the children learn the craft of fishing from their fathers and their uncles.

For most of the year the fishermen work alone or in family groups of two or three boats. But in the season when migratory shoals of snappers, scad, horse mackerel and yellowtail nose their way along the shoreline, fishermen from all the nearby communities join together as a fleet. Scores of little boats or *lepa* detach themselves from the floating villages moored together by the shore and set off for a particular reef or coral bank to lay a

To the Bajau Laut, here in the Tawi-Tawi islands of the Sulu sea, the land has little meaning. Their whole life is with the sea.

Dynamiting fish is illegal because it kills *all* marine life; but nets are laborious. The divers wear homemade goggles of wood and glass.

Boats are as much homes as are huts. The men fold the nets, a woman spreads shark and stingray on the roof of nipah palm to dry in the sun.

After decapitating his shark, this Bajau Laut will share the head among his friends and sell the body and fins to Chinese traders from Bongao.

trap for the approaching shoals. Every family on every boat brings its own gill net and these are strung together like an underwater fence. On the surface the mammoth net is buoyed up by cork floats, and under the water it is weighted down with shell sinkers.

The fishermen work together to drag the huge trap into a semi-circle – 200 or perhaps 300 yards across – and then take their places in an arc of boats, drawn up over the open water facing the nets. Each village has chosen a leader for today, and all eyes are on these leaders – *nakura* – who will give the signal to begin. The fishermen wait quietly but with great excitement. The great fishing drive is vital to the livelihood of every community. It is also the spectacle the Bajau Laut most love to watch.

The *nakura* give the signal and the *lepa* move forward, tightening the circle. On board the families pound the gunwales of their boat or beat the water with long poles. The noise is sudden and deafening. The *nakura* must judge the precise moment to start the hullaballoo, or the shoal might veer away instead of into the net. And they must be quick to give the signal to shoot the final wall of net over the mouth of the circle the instant they see inside the dark mass of flailing fish, driven before the fleet. When the haul of fish has been safely landed the *nakura* will divide it fairly, and must see to it that none of their followers cheat or become embroiled in fights with fishermen from other settlements.

No institutions bind the villages together, and the Bajau Laut form a distinct society only in that they have in common a way of life that centers exclusively around the sea, and speak related dialects of Samal. Their number is not known precisely – probably between 20,000 and 30,000 – and they are fragmented into hundreds of independent villages in the southern Philippines, in north eastern Borneo and over a large area of eastern Indonesia. But their way of life is distinctive, different from that of the other island people who share these coastlines.

The Bajau Laut village may be merely a flotilla of small fishing boats that regularly come together at a single anchorage. Or it may be a compact cluster of thatched wooden houses, so close to the shore that they have their feet in the sea. Except for their cemetery islands, where the dead of several villages have been buried over the centuries, most communities have no land or any other property ashore. From time to time an entire village may move on along the coast, and it is only these cemetery islands – and the notion that the ancestors buried there maintain an abiding and protective interest in the living – that gives the Bajau Laut any permanent bearings on the land.

Their life is regulated by tides, currents and the seasonal movement of fish. The daily cycle of night and day, sunrise and sunset, takes second place to the exigencies of the sea. And so to westerners, accustomed to

The monsoon rain sweeps the boat settlement of Tungkalang. The widely ramified family links involve the people in communal tasks.

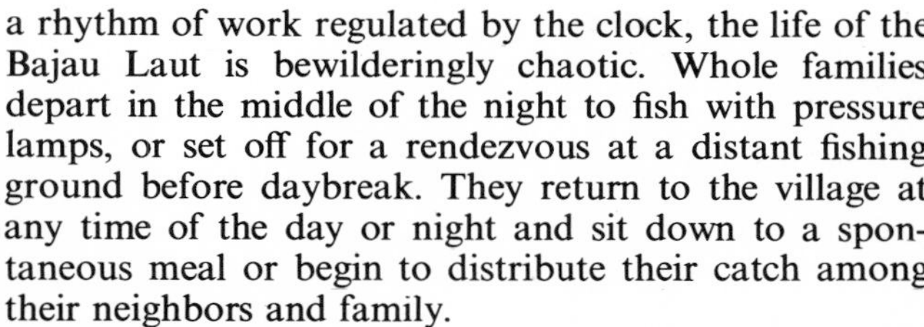

A family watch over their new baby boy, born four hours ago. Life is ruled by the moon. Bajau Laut seldom know their age nor what year it is.

a rhythm of work regulated by the clock, the life of the Bajau Laut is bewilderingly chaotic. Whole families depart in the middle of the night to fish with pressure lamps, or set off for a rendezvous at a distant fishing ground before daybreak. They return to the village at any time of the day or night and sit down to a spontaneous meal or begin to distribute their catch among their neighbors and family.

The fishermen land most of their catch by netting the fish in gill nets made by hand from cotton twine and natural fibers. But they use a great number of other divers fishing methods as well, reflecting the infinite variety of marine life that surrounds them. At night they fish for skate, porpoises and devil fish which they spear by the light of lanterns. Reef cod, bream and parrot fish they net or catch in snares or with handlines. Boats also carry spear guns and harpoon guns, poisons and explosives.

A fishing trip may last one or two days or several weeks, though the Bajau Laut seldom travel further than 40 miles from their home fishing grounds. The wooden *lepa* as well as being a fine sailing boat – with a mast stepped well forward, a four-cornered white sail and sometimes outriggers to steady it – is also a well equipped home. At night the family shelters under a roof of plaited nipah palm supported on a framework of bamboo. By day, when the *lepa* is under sail, the cover is rolled up and stowed away. Food and water for the voyage are stored in the stern, and there the meals are prepared. The Bajau Laut eat only fish and vegetables: they regard the meat of land animals as unclean.

All food other than fish and the few wild fruits they can gather the Bajau Laut must buy from their neighbors. They trade part of their catch for agricultural staples – such as cassava and yams – for nipah matting or for pots and pans and knives made in the local smithies. Trading relations with their coastal neighbors have not always been so amicable as they are now. In the past the Bajau Laut were persistently raided by outsiders, who stole property and took the fishermen as slaves. Against these raids the village headmen sought the protection of a political patron or *datu*, offering privileged trading rights in exchange, and binding themselves to work for him from time to time as pilots or as pearl divers. Thus they became linked – in a peripheral way – with the central administration of the Sulu state. But they soon learnt that if they were to receive protection from raiders they must resign themselves to being exploited. Since the decline of the Tausang sultanate and the development of a commercial market for fish, their economy is less politically entrammeled, and they trade largely for cash. But the legacy of conflict and suspicion persists. They continue to mistrust their neighbors, and the neighbors continue to call the Bajau Laut the *lawaquan* or the *palaqau* – both terms of abuse. The fishermen remain on the margins of society.

It is the custom for a bride to look grave on her wedding day and for the faces of bride and groom to be painted with chalk and charcoal.

Their villages are transient but they are vital to the life of the Bajau Laut. The Bajau Laut originally lived solely on their boats, but more recently they have been setting up more or less temporary settlements on shore, and now, as well as its *lepa*, nearly every family owns or shares a house where it returns between voyages. These houses are small – no more than one large room – supported six or eight feet above the sea on hardwood piles. Inside the family sleeps and entertains guests on ceremonial occasions. Around the room there are boxes and shelves where the family keeps all its personal belongings, and outside there is a separate kitchen built onto the front of the house. Outside, daily family life goes on in the open air on the wide landing stage at the front of every house. Planks and catwalks join the platforms in front of nextdoor houses and make up a network of thoroughfares through the village. Here the villagers pause to gossip, or gather in the evening to smoke, chew betel and tell endless tales about the sea.

The villagers are linked too by interlocking ties of kinship. Each man or woman has his *dampalanakan,* involving both his own and his wife's grandparents and all their descendants. The obligations that bind him to this large family range from helping to land a haul of fish to contributing to a relative's bride-price. Most marriages are arranged within the *dampalanakan* when the couple are still children – perhaps by cunning parents who have the bride-price in mind. This means that the *dampalanakan* is more closely bound together while the property is kept in the family. More than 80 per cent of all marriages are arranged between cousins, although these are traditionally prohibited unless their parents will pay a ritual fine to placate the spirits, and thus divert the spiritually harmful effects of the union. No man can count all the people of his village among his own *dampalanakan* but the community is highly interrelated and the family groups constantly overlap. Villagers in general consider themselves as kin.

Every household has its nominal head – the senior man of the *dampalanakan.* But his sons and daughters and their children who share his house all have their own income and property – their own *lepa* – and the influence of the headman depends more on his ability as a fisherman than on his title. He can only truly lead the *dampalanakan* or call upon the family to share his ventures if his skill is well respected. An old man of the Bajau Laut has few possessions to hand on to his sons (traditionally his boat was dismantled at his death and reshaped as his coffin) and so he has no material hold over them.

The groom has come to take his wife to her new home. Most Bajau Laut are nominally Muslim and the groom wears a *keffiyeh* headcloth from Arabia.

A man sick with malaria is joined by another whom he offended. The sick man goes into a trance while the other begs the spirits' forgiveness.

All Bajau Laut have a common duty to maintain the goodwill of the spirits. Flags have been set up on a rock inhabited by spirits to please them.

By the time of his death the old man has usually given away most of his other property – musical instruments or jewelry – to his sons and daughters at their wedding feasts. His personal possessions are buried with him. Wealth is measured in terms of labor: a successful headman is a successful fisherman himself, who can attract and hold many followers. As the headman grows older his sons break away to set up households of their own, usually as close as possible to their father's home. He remains at the center of the cluster of adjoining family houses, but his influence grows weaker and weaker as the last remaining son or daughter (usually the youngest) takes over the management of his house.

When a man grows too old to work a full day in the *lepa* he may turn his attention to the affairs of the community, as an elder or expert in ritual, or as a councillor to the village headman. The headman is elected by the elders to administer the law according to custom, and nowadays he must also fulfil the role of tax collector for the local authorities, and recorder of births and deaths. Once he has been chosen the headman serves the community until he dies, fulfilling the role of judge and mediator when disputes occur between the villagers. However his judgement has no legal status – he has no police to enforce it. If he is obeyed it is from respect for his knowledge of the laws and traditions of the Bajau Laut and for his superior qualities of fairness and impartiality. And he is seldom disobeyed.

Every villager shares with the headman the responsibility of safeguarding the peace of the community. Spiritually as well as materially each man's well-being depends on the well-being of his village. In a world full of danger the village must be preserved as a sanctuary from hazards both natural and supernatural. Ignorance or improper behavior can jeopardize this sanctuary and turn the village into a world of chaos and calamity. Ritual describes such disaster in terms of heat: the world will be made hot, filled with illness, accidents and death. All must take care not to invoke such chaos.

The Bajau Laut are nominally Muslim – though neighboring people call them pagan – and worship the god of Islam. But they fear most the *saitan,* spirits who are omnipresent in their lives. Myriads of *saitan* infest the universe, and if they are angered – or through sheer malice – they burden the people with illness and misfortune.

Two people are particularly responsible for maintaining the serenity of the community, the *imam,* who is the guardian of religious law and ritual and the *jin* who is the emissary of the *saitan.* The *imam* is expert both in secular morals and customs and in the proscriptions of Islam. He presides over rites of circumcision, at marriages and at funerals. Funeral rites follow the laws of Islam. The body is washed and covered in a shroud and buried within 24 hours. After the burial there are prayers and a funeral feast. Until the rites are over the dead man's

Cemeteries like this on Sitangkai are shared by neighboring communities and are the only significant land bearings for the Bajau Laut.

A *lepa* stands in dry dock being cleaned by its owner with burning coconut fronds which remove salt and seaweed from the hull.

This girl's home is Tungkalang, a community of nearly a hundred stilt houses and *lepas* around a tiny sandbar which almost disappears at high tide.

kin are in a state of jeopardy. They must avoid all major undertakings – boat building or fishing voyages – and pray at the graveside, which is surrounded by a wooden paling and marked with a wooden tablet. The cemetery is a dangerous place to linger, as the ghosts of those who died too soon, or who led a life of violence remain there to haunt the living. The *imam* stays there with the relatives, leading their prayers. He also conducts the *magmaulud* celebrations, when the whole village joins in a ceremony of thanksgiving for good fortune or for someone's recovery from illness.

The *jin* on the other hand is in contact with the darker powers, and, with the help of his spirit familiars, he can divine the order that governs the spirit world, and he advises his village how to avoid the wrath of the *saitan*. Both the *iman* and the *jin* may demand sacrifice from anyone who ignores their precepts. A breach of the moral or religious laws is punished by a fine. For offences which have incurred the anger of the *saitan* a sacrifice must be made.

The Bajau Laut have many *jin* (or shamans) – at least one to every two or three households – and their role is deeply embedded in village tradition. They are men and women whom the spirits have called, and who have undergone a rigorous initiation – involving a period of sickness – and a long training before they can master the spirit world. They are most often called upon to cure illness, for which the *saitan* are always held responsible. And they also conduct religious rites, particularly the *magigak* when they invoke the spirits to renew their supernatural powers. Through the night the *jin* dance to a frenzy of excitement, calling on their own special spirit or familiar to possess their bodies, and to strengthen the collective defenses of the village.

Sometimes hordes of wandering and malevolent spirits penetrate these defenses and infect the bodies of the villagers. Only the *jin* can oust the *saitan* and cure the raging epidemic. He makes a circuit of the village stopping at each house and summoning the evil powers to follow him. Then he locks the spirits into carved wooden effigies and places them aboard the *pamatulikan,* a spirit ship specially constructed from cloth, and supplied with food and water by all the villagers. The boat is equipped for a voyage and as the invocation ends, the spirits are bid to depart, and continue their wanderings elsewhere. Then the *pamatulikan* is towed out to the open sea and set adrift.

Through their skilful exploitation of the wealth of the sea the Bajau Laut have clung to their autonomous position on the margins of society. But they feel themselves threatened, both by the neighbors who have molested them in the past and by the spirits who menace the peace of every day. The Bajau Laut counter these threats by their stable and pragmatic attitude to life, their responsibility one to another and their faith in the value of hard work.

Planks and causeways link up the houses but boys find stilts more fun for walking through the murky, reeking water of low tide.

People of Manila and the northern highlands

Manila is the principal city and only true metropolitan center of the Republic of the Philippines. It is a city which brings together Filipinos who are an oriental people, and westerners – mostly Americans. There is a mixing of the two cultures, for there has been a long history in Manila of two, or even three different peoples living side by side. But the mixing is harsh; there are jagged edges where the American ways are taken up by Filipinos. Great estates that had once been owned by Spaniards or the Church during the time of Spanish rule passed into the hands of a few Filipino families after the Americans took over. The families behaved with no less greed and arrogance than their predecessors. One American at the time commented, 'The idea that public office is a public trust has not been planted in the Filipino mind by experience.' The Americans appeared to have entrusted power to a class of Filipinos whose economic interest lay in misusing that power. Under the exploitation of such men, many Filipino peasants rebelled in the 1930s, just as they had risen before against their Spanish oppressors and as they would again, as communists, after World War II.

Manila has had four centuries of life. Those years, 300 under a harsh Spanish administration, then 40 years under the Americans and the years of World War II under the Japanese, have served to create a city that is sometimes described as brutal, corrupt and sickening. There is a bed of violence in Manila that is undeniable; a recent American research team showed that there was a murder ever hour in the Philippines. But if there is a disease in Manila, the infection was caught long ago and has remained in the body ever since, sometimes to break out violently. Even Manila's beginnings were tainted with death.

In 1570, Captain Miguel Lopez de Legaspi, the leader of the first successful Spanish colonizing expedition to the Philippines, heard reports of an important trading center in the region of Manila Bay on the island of Luzon. The place was described to him as fertile and abundantly supplied with food, and possessing an estimated 80,000 Moros (Muslim Filipinos) in its environs. Legaspi was immediately interested and dispatched his chief lieutenant to find the place. The lieutenant was successful and captured the two fortified settlements of Moros which lay in Manila bay at the mouth of the Pasig river. The following year Legaspi brought up his full force and began to build the future capital of the Philippine colony. He inaugurated the construction of 150 wooden buildings for his soldiers, laid out the city across the Pastig river with a government house, church and monastery, and rebuilt the fortifications. The walls were 40 feet thick and the Spanish governor ruled by the cross and the sword.

The Catholic cross impressed the Filipinos more than any sword or pistol would ever do. The early Franciscan friars came to be hated for their avarice; they were burnt

Philippines

Hundreds of thousands gather every Easter to watch men pull a cross through Manila at the feast of the Black Virgin of Quiapo.

Each year at Pampanga, north of Manila, a chosen penitent is given the honor of being nailed to a cross in fulfilment of a vow.

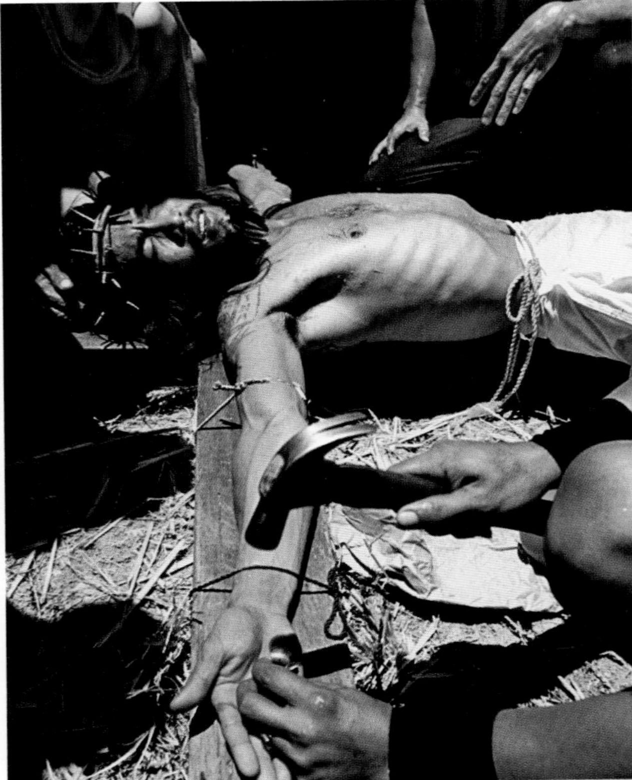

During Holy Week devout flagellants have their backs scratched with a knife to intensify their penitence and suffering.

(Right) The people of Quiapo, a district of Manila, celebrate the Festival of the Black Nazarene, their patron saint, in January.

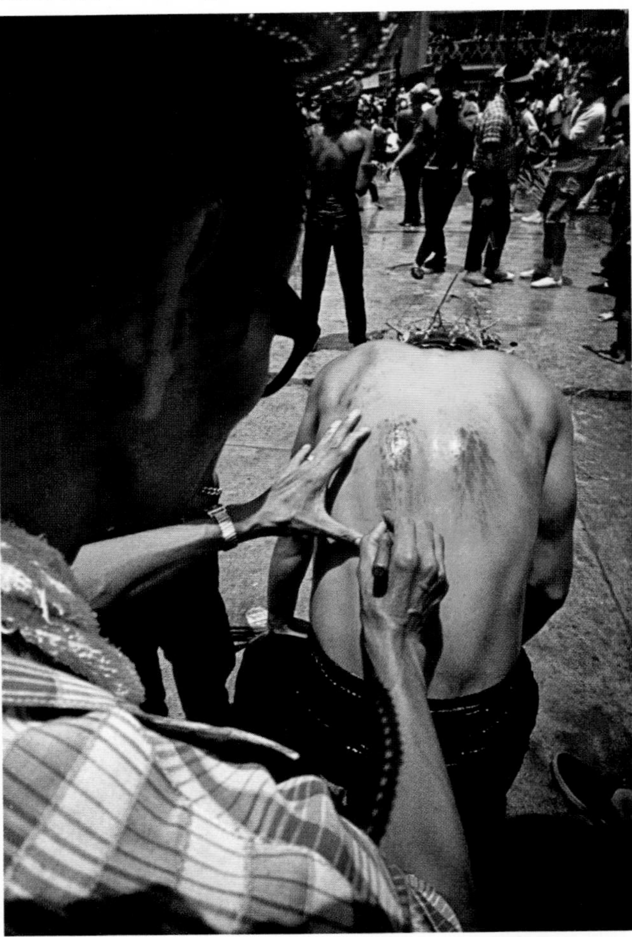

alive by the peasants during rebellions. And yet the Filipinos were quick and lasting converts to the Catholic faith. Today in Manila, hundreds of thousands gather for the feast of the Black Virgin of Quiapo, to watch a row of men pulling a heavy cross through the streets, each man wearing a towel about his head to honor the towel handed to Jesus on the cross; and each man barefoot despite the broken glass that litters the streets of Manila. Filipinos who have stayed awake in night clubs or plotting murder, go on to mass a few hours later.

For the Spanish, almost 400 years ago, Manila was the focal point of trade between China and Mexico. This trade was called the Manila Galleon Trade. Japanese and Chinese traders had long been active in these waters. And the Spanish, finding no significant spice markets in their new Philippine colony, turned to the China trade. The Manila Spanish soon became almost totally dependent on the Chinese traders who brought in a constant stream of oriental goods. In exchange the Chinese took away some Filipino domestic products and the silver bullion which came to the Spanish from Mexico. Even at this time, a few favored Filipinos were admitted to this profitable enterprise. And the region around Manila Bay became a wedge of Chinese and Filipino intermarriage; it was here that the Filipino culture gathered elements of both Spanish and Chinese cultures.

In Manila the Chinese worked as skilled craftsmen, as

Flagellants take part in the Good Friday procession through Manila. Some in a frenzy prostrate themselves at the feet of the crowd

The quiet Pasig river flows through one of the world's most violent cities where passers-by barely turn to look at a body in the gutter.

(Center) Veepneys, converted US army surplus jeeps custom built to any requirement, are Manila's own answer to commuter transport problems.

Some Filipino families became rich after the US gained control of the Philippines; their descendants now form a wealthy élite.

The US has given the Philippines Labor Day on May 1st, a workingman's holiday when the unions parade through Manila.

commercial traders and trade financiers. They quickly filled in the vacuum created by the sudden appearance of urban commercial activity. Historically, the Filipinos in Manila had never engaged in true commercial trading, and the Spanish did not encourage them. They did not respond to the new opportunities. This was left to the Chinese who eventually extended their operations into the hinterland. But there was, at the same time, frequent intermarriage between the Chinese and the Filipinos.

From the very beginning of the Spanish period in Manila, there was relatively little contact between Filipinos and Spaniards. Most of the Filipinos anyway remained rural, and the only lasting and effective contact between the two peoples was through the Spanish clergy. Some priests learned the native languages and performed their rituals, ceremonies and services in the native tongue. It has been a popular illusion that Spanish became the language of the Philippines. It is probable that even towards the end of the 19th century, no more than 10 per cent spoke Spanish fluently. But with the creation of urban centers, and with commercial prosperity, this did encourage Filipinos to settle in the towns. There were, however, and still are many peoples on the island of Luzon who have resisted the pull to Manila. The Bontoc and Ifugao tribes of the mountains of northern Luzon are prime examples. These tribes, and many others, were large enough and possessed a sufficiently cohesive culture to maintain their separate identity. Nevertheless, Manila continued to grow. Some of the earliest references to the town speak of a population of some 30,000 to 40,000. The leading Spanish and Filipino families lived within the fortified part of the town. A sector outside the town housed the Chinese, Japanese, Indonesians and other Asiatic people who visited or lived in Manila. A large Filipino population gathered in the suburbs, many of whom worked for the Spanish.

The suburban sectors of Manila were never, at this stage, subject to formal planning, but there were several centers sited at different points. Each contained a plaza, a church, government buildings, a core of residential houses and extensive shanty slums. In time these places grew together, overlapping, to form the larger part of Manila. Stone churches, government buildings and many of the high-class houses were repeatedly destroyed between the 16th and 18th centuries by earthquakes, and the Filipino sectors often burned. Frequent rebuilding was necessary. By the late 19th century, there were rules which required all private residences in Manila to be built of wood above the first storey. In its early period, Manila was often described as a dull city. The primary business center grew up north of the Pasig river as a crowded and drab area. Though a few wharfs and quays were built along the mouth of the river, it was really too narrow and too shallow to serve as a port. Instead its facilities were used for inter-island trade. The flat bay shore and the shallow bay waters required offshore anchorages, and passengers and cargo were brought ashore from the ocean-going ships in lighters.

In the mid-19th century, Manila was a large city with a population of more than 200,000. It had many centers apart from the one within the old Spanish fortifications, and this decentralization continued until the end of the century. But this period in Manila's history was also a time of change. The Spanish had already lost all their colonies in America except for Cuba and Puerto Rico. The Cuban and the Philippine rebellions came at about the same time. In 1896 the Spanish authorities executed José Rizal, a great Filipino writer, scholar and patriot. This and a hundred other killings throughout the Philippines ignited a revolt. There were hideous cruelties on both sides. The Spanish tortured suspected Filipino insurgents and then put them in subterranean cells in which they drowned at high tide. Filipinos seized the hated Franciscan friars and burned them slowly over fires. The Spaniards were eventually forced to make terms with the rebels. It was also at this dangerous time, in 1898, that the US battleship *Maine* was blown up in Havana harbor in Cuba, an action which brought America and Spain to war. The US fleet was ordered to the Philippines where it destroyed the Spanish fleet and captured the city of Manila.

An American army was sent to the Philippines, but in spite of this, the country's future remained undecided throughout 1898. There was an army of Filipino nationalists who wanted complete independence, both from Spain and from America. In the US there was uncertainty. A naval commander said that the Filipinos were 'superior in intelligence and more capable of self government than the Cubans'. But a combination of other interests in America favored annexation of the islands. One newspaper voiced a crude reasoning: 'The Filipino is treacherous and deceitful. Besides, we want his country.' In December 1898 at the Spanish American peace talks in Paris, the Philippines were transferred to US sovereignty. The Filipino army commander held his troops back, hoping that the treaty would not be ratified in the US senate. But the American expansionists succeeded and the treaty was passed. For the Filipinos, as a Manila senator once remarked, 300 years in a Spanish convent had ended – and 40 years in Hollywood had begun. In February 1899, a nervous American sentry shot and killed a Filipino officer. The subsequent war was to last four years and cost 250,000 lives.

The Philippines suffered the rare experience of being governed within 50 years by two different powers, with different political systems, different faiths, different cultures and even different languages. Manila, always the focus of change, lost its claim to be like an old Seville and became an aspiring Chicago. To the country as a whole, the Americans brought mass education, control of disease and a re-organization of the administration. Many of these reforms, however, were frustrated or

Lavish parties are held almost every night in Forbes Park, Manila's wealthiest suburb, known as millionaires' row.

wrecked by the few Filipino families who assumed far greater responsibility after the Spanish were gone. Rich families acquired a large measure of control of banking, the courts and the Civil Service. They appropriated millions of dollars and effectively ruined the American plans for land reform.

Then came World War II and the Japanese invasion. The Filipinos proved to be the most ferocious of enemies for Japan. Throughout the islands, Filipino resistance fighters waged a constant guerrilla war against the Japanese. The thousands of weapons flown in by Americans were put to good use – but those weapons are still in use today for criminal or political purposes. Manila itself was one of the most damaged cities by the end of the war, and killing and torture had become such a commonplace that Filipinos had acquired a fatalistic attitude towards life. This undoubtedly has contributed to the violence in Manila, a city where people scarcely turn their heads to look at a corpse in the street. The underworld has a genuine air of America, but an antique America of the late-night gangster movie. There are scar-faced crooks with their bodyguards meeting in murky nightclubs; tommy-gun battles fought from fast cars; corrupt policemen and cynical, whisky drinking reporters. The city is softer than Chicago, but small brown Filipinos often die through gun-shot wounds.

In central Luzon, the reaction to American influence – America still wields a powerful economic force despite Philippine independence – is expressed by the rebellion of insurgent groups like the Huks. These are communist gangs who raise money by extortion, blackmail and theft. Among them, crime becomes confused with politics, and politics with crime. And yet to go further north into the mountains of northern Luzon, among the pagan tribes who have, for 400 years, resisted Christianization, the political activist is replaced by the passive rice farmer who nonetheless refuses all temptations of modern Philippine society.

The streams and rivers which flow from the high slopes of these northern mountain ranges, grow into the 120 mile long Cagayan river. In the early 16th century, this waterway made travel into the northern interior of Luzon easy for Spanish explorers, missionaries and *encomenderos* or men to whom the Spanish Crown had allotted districts from which they could collect taxes. But despite this, the rugged mountainous country and hostility of the tribes allowed the Spanish to make little impression. Today, the region is inhabited by some eight distinct groups of people who altogether number more than 300,000. Although they share many linguistic and cultural features, there are also wide differences in some aspects of agriculture. This may be accounted for by the huge differences in climate throughout the northern mountains. In the northerly cordillera, the mountain peaks are low and the land is covered in dense tropical rain forest. The rivers are navigable and effectively bind isolated communities together. By contrast, the southern cordillera mountain peaks rise to more than 9,000 feet, and the rivers which cut through scrub and pine forest are fast and unnavigable. The most pronounced difference between the tribes who live here is their form of rice farming. On the southern slopes the Ifugao, Bontoc, Southern Kalinga, Ibaloy, Kankanay and Tinguian tribes irrigate the terraces they have built on the slopes and cultivate wet rice. On the northern and eastern slopes, the Gaddang, Northern Kalinga and Isneg tribes are slash-and-burn, dry rice farmers.

The way of life of these mountain farmers seems a thousand years away from the Filipinos who live in Manila. The spectacular mountain terraces of the Ifugao tribe have been carved into the slopes, each terrace supported by a long stone-work step, and from a distance the ascending terraces climb into the sky like a green, velvet staircase. Sometimes the Ifugao farmers stop the flow of water into the terraces in order to plant the first seedlings. Then, later, 12 inches of water will surround the growing crop. The terraces are centuries old and are used season after season. And around these terraces and water sources, there have evolved elaborate systems of law and inheritance for the people. To maintain his claim to a particular terrace, a man may be asked to trace the line of his descent from the original owner who may have lived ten or twelve generations before. The Ifugao live in small hamlets close to their rice terraces and kinship is the basis of all relationships between people. In the case of a dispute over ownership the most influential members of the kin-group – who will also be the wealthiest and possess the most livestock, beads and Chinese ceramics – will negotiate a settlement.

In contrast, the Bontoc, who are also wet rice farmers, live in much larger villages which are divided into territorial units called *ato*. Councils of older men preside over the affairs of every *ato* and, in the days of headhunting, it was they who decided on revenge expeditions and demands for compensation. There is a tendency for boys and girls within the *ato* to think of each other as brother and sister and so not consider marrying. And then among the Tinguian, another group of wet rice farmers, the villages are still larger and authority is vested in a *lakay* or headman. The *lakay* is advised by what might be described as an aristocratic class of wealthy men. Tinguian parents arrange marriages for their children and divorce is impossible to obtain.

The social structure of these tribal settlements of wet rice cultivators is however far more complex than that of the dry rice cultivators, the Gaddang, Northern Kalinga and Isneg tribes of the northern mountain slopes, slash-and-burn agriculturalists to whom the control of land is relatively unimportant. A man's status in any community is achieved not by inheritance of rice terraces or other forms of wealth, but through his own achievements. Before the American administration stamped out headhunting early in the 20th century, leadership among these tribes was reserved exclusively for successful headhunters. There is little need to recall descent from distant ancestors and, indeed, it is believed that speaking of a dead relative can incite the spirit of that person to cause misfortune in the family. Female spirit mediums often place the responsibility for particular inflictions on the spirit of a dead relative who has been offended by a careless word or deed.

Little more than 250 miles separates these mountain tribes from Manila. It does not take long to step from the Catholic faith of Manila's Filipinos to the superstitions of pagan Isneg tribesmen. The contrast between the subsistence rice farming of these tribes and the industrial and commercial activities of Manila is vivid. But some things are inconsistent with the notion that urban life is closer to the civilized ideal. In Manila there is the all too frequent practice of wives giving their unfaithful husbands a 'Filipino haircut' which means cutting their throats. Among the mountain tribes, headhunting has long been out of favor.

A harassed businessman enjoys a peaceful game of golf near Manila. Filipinos have adopted American sports like baseball, horse-racing and boxing.

(Bottom) The rich play polo while ordinary Filipinos prefer cockfighting or *arnis de mano*, a type of fencing using two sticks.

Peoples of Indonesia

From the earliest times Indonesia, which lies between Asia and Australia, between the Pacific and Indian Oceans, has been a meeting place of peoples and cultures. One of the oldest fossils of primitive man was found in Java. Many peoples moved to the Indonesian islands from the Asian mainland. The earliest of them seem to have been related to present-day Melanesians, and they killed or subdued the indigenous peoples. The next migrant people was the Negrito race of which a few representatives survive not only in this area, but in other parts of South Asia and Oceania. Then came Austronesian speaking peoples from southern China who were good sailors and traveled from Madagascar to the farthest eastern islands in the Pacific; they were the ancestors of present-day Malay-Polynesians. Most of the many languages of Indonesia are Austronesian, as is Malay, of which modern Indonesian is a variant.

The Malay immigrants brought with them a highly developed and highly productive system of wet rice cultivation, and the complex hierarchical social structure that evolved from it. Both became most firmly established in the fertile land of central Java. Elsewhere the Malays grew rice in forest clearings, which needed less organization, supported only small groups, and produced less complex and less hierarchical social structures. Java has to this day a kind of cultural ascendancy over most of the other islands – at the least there is some sort of cultural opposition.

This rice growing culture had established itself by a period two thousand years ago, and most Indonesians lived in small fairly democratic village communities, growing rice, fishing, worshipping ancestors and spirits, and perhaps beginning to trade. At some time in the third century Indonesia came under Indian influences, and adopted first Hinduism, and about two centuries later Buddhism as well. In Indonesia both religions and their priests adapted themselves to coexist peacefully together, avoiding India's bitter religious conflicts.

Meanwhile trade increased. Many traders – Indians and Persians – stopped at the Indonesian islands, especially at the Moluccas, to buy spices, pepper and precious woods on their way to China. In this way Islam came to Indonesia in the 12th century AD. Today 90 per cent of all Indonesians are Muslims, though Bali, parts of Lombok and some parts of western Java are Hindu areas. The Islamic period lasted until about 1800, giving way to Portuguese influences and the Dutch colonial period which ended with World War II when the Japanese occupied Indonesia, and made some lasting impressions. Today animism exists side by side with ancestor worship, Hinduism and Buddhism.

Rather Indonesia has to deal with the new and urgent problems of overpopulation. Most Indonesians work on the land – occupying less than half an acre each, and the earth is not rich. Many of the 3,000 islands cannot support large numbers of people, who tend to concentrate in the more fertile areas of western Sumatra, the Lesser Sunda islands and Java, where there are sometimes three or four thousand people to the square mile on average. Wet rice cultivation *(sawah)* is done with plows and harrows often of wood and drawn by water buffalo and oxen, and the women and children do the planting and weeding manually. In less fertile areas the Indonesians clear virgin forest land and plant rice in dry fields: but this exhausts the soil, which is often not given time to recover. The Javanese cultivate dry fields, which is less productive. Most farmers are too poor to buy fertilizers or better equipment and have no extra land for commercial crops. Though peasant-farming is labor-intensive, many Indonesians are underemployed, and have to practise various handicrafts or seek work on plantations as well. So Indonesia has much excess labor which is both inefficient and immobile and peasant agriculture cannot support the growing population.

Indonesia's cash crops, produced on estates and on smallholdings are rubber, copra, sugar, coffee, tea and tobacco. Both rubber plants and coconut trees thrive on poor soil, and can survive neglect or inefficiency: the other cash crops need more attention and tend to be cultivated in Indonesia. Though there are substantial oil deposits coal resources are running out, and iron ore supplies are small and inconveniently distributed. In the Riau archipelago and in North Sumatra there are good bauxite deposits, and there are other minerals such as copper, manganese and tin – which is an important export. However, heavy industry is unlikely to develop on a large scale. Consumer goods industries are more promising: Indonesian silverware and batik are world-famous, and there is a market for Indonesian art, like Balinese sculpture. Nonetheless Indonesia relies heavily on foreign aid.

About a tenth of the population of Indonesia today lives in towns, like Djakarta, Surabaya or Medan, leading westernized lives, wearing western clothes, and seeing western films. The rest live in the country, usually

Bussus, hermaphrodite priests, here attending a harvest festival, are the third immortal sex. They came to earth on a rainbow.

in close-knit village communities with highly developed and much respected systems of values. Now in fact there is a great opposition between town and country. 'Rural' virtually means 'uneducated' from a city dweller's point of view. The Javanese language makes, for example, no distinction between 'stupid' and 'uneducated'. Especially in hierarchical Java, the aristocracy in the past lived in Court Towns like Jogyakarta and Surakarta, and as the upholders of courtly manners formed a class called the *priyayi*, into which the lower-born intelligentsia were gradually assimilated in the 19th century. The *priyayi* always believed that their function was service to the state, and this function has never been lost, and the upper class of today is urban dwelling, educated, important in government or professional life and probably well connected socially. There is an urban middle class of clerks and tradesmen who enjoy greater prestige than uneducated country laborers.

Most people live in the country. In each village members of the community share responsibility for the common welfare and for public order. Individuals, and individual property are secondary concerns – in many parts of Indonesia the community controls land use and ownership. Despite the variety of linguistic, cultural and religious idiosyncracies of particular areas or islands values tend to be similar in all village life. The most fundamental value is loyalty to the ties of kinship. This deep-rooted feeling perhaps explains the amount of nepotism in Indonesian public life. Close to this is the Javanese ideal of *gotong royong*, or mutual aid, which is a political catch phrase as well as a felt belief. It is evident both in villages where labor is exchanged, and in city life where services (and not fees) are exchanged.

Common to most villages is an absence of any western sense of time, or its value, and consequently, of planning. Work and leisure, for example, are not separate. And the products of work are shared, not necessarily equally – indeed more usually not – but always so as to provide for those in need. In most villages as in cities, women hold a high position, much higher than in India or China.

Between different ethnic groups there are considerable differences of attitude: Javanese values are clearly distinguishable, and often opposed, to other Indonesian values. Their culture has been centralized and monarchic, and they tend to despise trade: and show less commercial initiative than more democratic peoples.

For any particular Indonesian, there are two sets of loyalties: one to either Muslim or western attitudes, the other to his ethnic group and these affinities determine his social mobility. A man of 'western' attitude will have something in common with most other westernized people all over the archipelago, but much less with a villager from his own part of the country.

Similarly the arts in Indonesia today are either broadly westernized, or predominantly traditional. Westernized art is realistic, produced by individual artists, and inspired by nationalism. Traditional art, on the other hand, is idealized, produced by anonymous artists, based on traditional beliefs and varies from area to area. Only the Malay and Javanese peoples have any long tradition of literature, though all groups have forms of singing and story telling, like the Malay *patun* or short verses. These recount heroic epics, with stock characters, like the mouse-deer, who represents the victory of cunning over might, the universal wise-clown figure.

Music, dancing and theater have remained completely traditional, varying greatly from island to island, and from group to group. The *krontjong*, a kind of stringed music introduced by the Portuguese in the 16th century is now so widespread that it is almost a national musical style. There are, too, many much older forms, like the Islamic drumming of Sumatra or the songs of Amboina which resemble Hawaiian music. Javanese *gamelan* orchestras are particularly famous. *Gamel* means hammer, and the orchestras are made of percussion instruments only. They are played at dances, functions or processions, or to accompany Javanese or Balinese shadow plays – *wayang kulit*. This is the most popular entertainment in Indonesia, and extremely old: shadow plays were known and popular in the year 1000. They were much influenced by Indian culture, but withstood Islam and the Dutch and in fact were used by nationalists to spread anti-Dutch propaganda. The magic and religious significance of the puppets cannot be overestimated. Even President Sukarno identified himself with one of the heroic stock characters, a lovable young prince of integrity and modesty called Gatutkacha. The puppets are flat and stylized following the Islamic prohibition of naturalistic art. They symbolise human attributes, in their roles and in their appearance.

Of the other arts, dancing is extremely highly developed, and has religious associations, and the same is true of Balinese stone sculpture, and of their distinctive wood carving, which is predominantly Hindu. Contemporary theater is much weaker, and the film industry has until recently uncritically parodied Hollywood.

Students in Bandung, Java, influenced by popular western films, have adopted the clothes and attitudes of western society.

Nias
Sumatra

A Nias war party sets out to attack a neighboring village. If victorious they will kill all the enemy warriors and take home the chief's head.

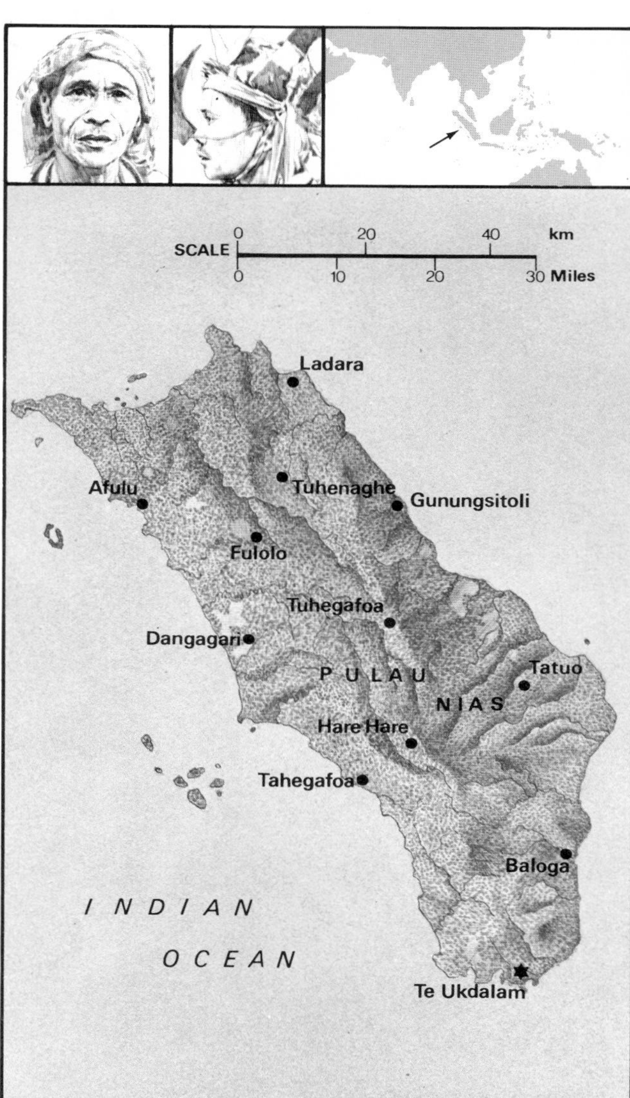

The life of the Nias islander is dominated by the great stone shapes that clutter his village square. An island 80 miles long by 30 wide lying to the south and west of central Sumatra, Nias has the purest megalithic culture in the world. The prestige and power of a Nias islander can be directly measured by the great stone shapes – striking in their solidity and simple beauty – that he has erected in his lifetime. In the Celebes, in the islands of Flores and Sumba and in parts of Polynesia there are people who have similar customs. But it is a further source of wonder that the people who most closely share the Nias culture are the Naga of mountainous Assam, thousands of miles away to the north-east of India.

Although some of them have the wavy, coarse, black hair, heavy eye-ridges and flat noses of the Veddoid people, the Nias islanders are of Malaysian stock. Most

As night falls, villagers in Hilisimaetano prepare to defend their homes. If they succeed in severing an enemy head, they lick the knife.

A pig is being ceremoniously slaughtered. Dutch colonial rulers were not entirely successful in saving slaves from the same ritual fate.

Men on Nias only reach an average height of 5 feet, yet boys must jump over a 7 foot high stone plinth before they can 'become men'

have the straight black hair and yellowish skin of the Malaysian people who probably came down from South China in about 2,000 BC. Their eyes are slit and their features delicate. Most are small – the men average just five feet in height. The Naga and the Nias people, however, must share some common origin – perhaps some millennia back. Archeologists reckon that at some time in the course of their migration they lived together as one people in the Irrawaddy valley, in what is now Burma.

In the less populous north of Nias, the land is flat and marshy. But in the south, where people are reputedly more energetic, the land is rocky and the islanders, for strategic reasons, live in hilltop villages. They are fierce and active warriors. Here in the south where the megalithic culture is most developed, you approach the villages by climbing up long stone staircases – the one in the village of Bawomatalowa has 700 steps. In the village square you are confronted with a maze of obelisks, dolmens – stone mushroom-shapes usually a couple of feet high – and *osaosa,* stone seats with fantastic representations of animal heads at one end and tails at the other. This army of stone stands between the village's two rows of houses that make the square. Old men like to sit here with their backs propped up against the cool stone on the shady side of the sturdy megaliths. And children weave and dart between the shapes, their bare feet slapping on the large stone paving slabs of the square. The dolmens were made for wives to dance upon – but children usurp the privilege. Each dolmen when struck gives out its own note, a percussion orchestra of stone.

But nobody treats the megaliths irreverently. Even the children can tell you the date and the founder of each monument. Many of the adults remember the feasts – 'feasts of merit', anthropologists call them – which, together with the sacrifice of large numbers of pigs and, in the old days, of humans too, entitled the feast-giver to raise the stone shapes as monuments to himself even in his own lifetime. Some of them are raised to commemorate the dead and to assist them in their struggle against evil spirits, but most are put up by the feast-giver to ingratiate himself, his family and his village, with the gods.

Each new feast and each consequent entitlement to a new bejeweled garment or new megalith means one more step up the ladder of fame, prestige and power – in this world as well as in the one beyond. The monuments are clearly phallic – they are a plea for continued fertility. The childless are forbidden to hold feasts of merit or to put up monuments. They are functional monuments whose beauty is quite incidental. For the patterns carved on the dolmens – rosettes, triangles, loops – are on the underside of the mushroom-shape: presumably for the eyes of the spirits only. But the islanders certainly give free rein to their imagination when they design their *osaosa,* the seats with a head one end and a tail the other upon which they sometimes set the chief and his wife after a large feast and carry them around the square. Sometimes the head has the horns of a deer, the nose of the rhinobird, eyes like windows, heavy earrings, a huge tongue and incisors, and the jaws and teeth of a crocodile. This fantastic array is the more exotic if the *osaosa* is dedicated to a wife. Most of the Nias stone objects are decorated with such sexual symbols as breast motifs, and the idols which rich men carve for their ancestors have grotesquely exaggerated genitalia. The 'feminine' dolmens, always constructed on behalf of a new bride, are often set together with phallic obelisks symbolizing the desire for fertility, both human and agricultural.

A man's first feast of merit will probably entitle him to receive gold jewelry, specially fashioned for himself and his wives. He has to slaughter some pigs and – although the Dutch colonial rulers almost stopped the habit – a slave as well. And when the jewels were ready, a slave – also soon to be disposed of – would have to wear them for a day or two in case the jealous spirits sent ill luck to the wearer. The next feast brings a man's wife the right to wear a gold dress and jacket, and a man may then have a three-headed *osaosa* built for him. One feast more, and he may carry a gold umbrella and wear a neck chain. He can now put up a pillar and a single-headed *osaosa.* But this time 100 pigs must die, not to mention another valuable slave. The next feast brings the wife a golden bracelet, after the slaughter of 30 pigs, and a stone bench under which a female slave would be buried. When a man's wife dies, she too is buried under the bench – with another slave who is called the wife's 'cushion'. To proceed to the next stage of his career the man builds a bench on a hilltop far from his village – and he has to slaughter another 100 pigs. He must kill 30 pigs for his next feast, which entitles him to furnish his own house with a stone bench. And before he dies he must give yet another feast to entitle him to a stone coffin. Two slaves meet their end at this point. One precedes the man to his grave and rids it of bad spirits – a bamboo tube from his mouth to the surface lets them out. And at death the man is accompanied by yet another slave buried on his right and known as his 'staff'. Few Nias islanders in fact reach the top rung of the ladder. Those who do, however, can be sure to die content.

Although Nias is divided into 37 districts, which are often at odds with each other, the fundamental unit of society is the village, presided over by a hereditary chieftain, whose mother must also be of a chiefly family. Chiefs are the gods incarnate and are called 'father' by their people. They alone are privileged to own slaves and wear gold. They often lend money or goods to commoners, who frequently fall deep into debt and then become their slaves. Slaves are otherwise acquired through war. It is not known to what extent, if any, the chiefs still exercise their rights over life and death. By Nias custom a chief is entitled, certainly, to sacrifice a slave simply when he has a new drum built for example.

(Over page) The chief's house in Bawomatalowa stands at the head of the paved square looking toward a stone staircase of 700 steps.

When the drum is beaten, say the islanders, the reverberation is the cry of the victim's soul within.

A chief would in fact usually be loath to lose his slaves, as they are expensive and he would tend to sacrifice only the aged or decrepit. There are certainly still signs of slave sacrifice. Most Nias pillars, for example, are topped by stone birds whose furled feathers form a small level platform – on which the severed head of a slave may securely perch. Slaves are always free to marry – and so increase their owner's supply. But bride-price is so high that many of the commoners, potential slaves, stay unmarried. The acme of the powers of a commoner would be election to the council of elders, which advises the chiefs and administers the law. There is an intricate civil and criminal code on Nias. Particularly harsh are the punishments for crimes involving women. If a man touches a woman's breast his hand will be cut off. Sexual mores are severely observed. A woman who becomes pregnant before marriage is killed, after she has been tortured – sometimes by ordeal under water – to confess the child's paternity. Virgin brides are twice as expensive as others. Young village girls sleep together in a house guarded at night by old women.

An activity in which commoners and chiefs both participate but from which slaves are excluded, is warfare.

A man's hand is cut off if he so much as touches a woman's breast. The bride at the wedding these women are going to is certain to be a virgin.

(Top) Children bring Nias islanders honor and status. Childless men may not hold feasts or put up monuments to themselves or to ancestors.

The ancient chief who had these memorial benches made will have died a happy man knowing that honor and power await him in the next world.

Wars are fought at night, usually between neighboring villages. All opposing warriors are killed, and assailing villagers collect the idols of the enemy village and heap them insultingly together underneath the enemy chief's house. As all houses are built on piles, to kill a personal enemy, you creep under his house and plunge your sword upwards through the floorboards on which he sleeps. Nias islanders are keen headhunters, for heads are accessory to many islanders' rites. The knife that severs the head must be licked by the victor – signifying perhaps a past bent for cannibalism.

It may surprise outsiders, to whom these customs may seem violent and cruel, that the villagers are peaceable among themselves. Feasting and raising megaliths may

be the most important events in their lives, but the villagers spend much more time quietly growing their crops and, when the harvest is over, hunting wild game together. They eat rice, sago, maize, taro, yams and coconuts, and the men drink palm wine. Pigs are a delicacy, and ritually slaughtered by stabbing. Then they are singed before the right part is meticulously allocated to the right person. The islanders like to eat chicken too, but before doing so offer the liver and feathers to the spirits. They hunt boar, deer, apes, boa constrictors, birds and fish, but never mice – for they contain ancestors' souls. Women may not eat monkey meat, and crocodiles are respected by all. They eagerly shoot owls, whose hoot brings flood. There is a fussy hunting etiquette. Before the hunters set out, tree spirits must be propitiated and nobody may sweep out the house, break crockery or ring gongs. Nor may there be any mention by name of the game that is hunted.

In a single house live at least one, but sometimes several, nuclear families. Houses are oval-shaped in the north and rectangular in the south. You enter a smart house through a stone gateway, but a ladder leads you up into most dwellings. Chiefs' houses are much larger than commoners' houses. Otherwise houses are laid out everywhere in the same way. The main room looks onto the square, with a fire at the back. The family sleeps behind a lattice screen, furthest from the square.

The large chiefs' houses, some of which are 70 feet high, although never of more than one storey, may take as long as five years to build. Before and after the house is built priests, whose calling is hereditary, make sacrifices inside the foundations. Drums are beaten to scare away spirits, the owner holds feasts, and his slaves roll pigs (which are later eaten) from the skeletal rooftop.

The core of the chief's house is a central pillar which flowers where it reaches the roof. His furniture is of stone or wood. There are chests, leaf mats, food baskets; clubs and lances, animal head trophies and pigs' jawbones along the walls. His pillows are made of wood.

Outside the house there is a *bale* – a small building that houses wooden ancestral idols and, on occasions, live guests. Nias islanders, like the Naga, closely combine spiritual and material affairs. Religion is never far from any aspect of their lives. The megaliths they so assiduously put up are for both ancestor spirits and the great gods – above all for Lowalangi of the sky who fights a devil figure. The Nias people have a trinity of gods who predestine the length of a man's life. They keep pots of 'breath' which they allocate in varied amounts to mortals. When your supply of breath runs out, you die. Many intricate details of Nias religion – the sacred cat, for instance, that helps guard the bridge that leads after death to heaven or hell – are identical to the beliefs of the Naga.

When he dies, the chief is placed on a stone platform and dressed in gold, with his eyes and nose blocked up. People wail, clang gongs, dance and feast. For four days they say his body is 'alive'. Then they bury him in a coffin which they call a boat. They find a spider near the grave – the chief reincarnate – and press it onto a waiting wooden idol. In this way they see his safe passage into the house of the idols.

Only by boat can you go from Sumatra to Nias and its 150,000 islanders. The place remains isolated, untouched in its megalithic purity. And it is strange and wonderful, in this jet age, that two so widely separated communities – one in the mountains of Assam, the other thousands of miles away in island Indonesia – should continue to attach the same fervent meaning to the creation of great stone shapes mysterious to other men.

Iban
Borneo

Tattoos are both decoration and status symbol. Only the bravest men have tattooed hands for that shows how many heads they have cut off.

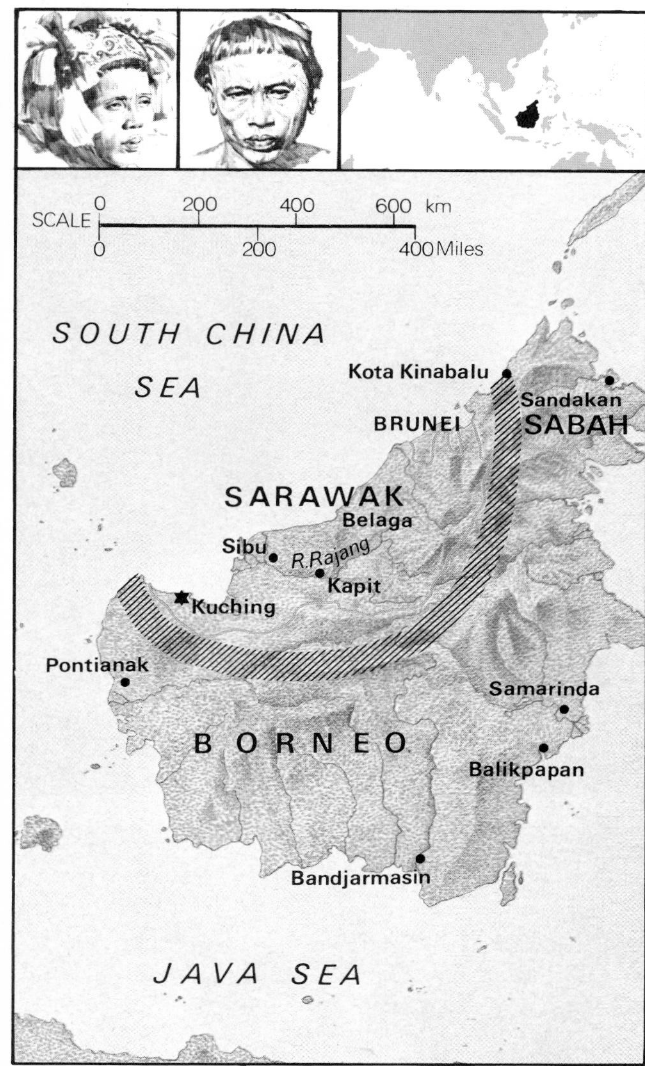

There are few roadways that lead inland from Borneo's coastlands. The forests sprawl for hundreds of miles, thick and green so that light from the glaring sun is scattered into leafy patterns and tumbles through the trees like a waterfall. But there are rivers. The forests are ribboned with them and these are the pathways. The Rajang river is one of these, running westward from the interior to the northern coast of Sarawak. And on the Rajang lies the small town of Kapit which is the trading center of the Iban.

The Iban are a large tribe. Their numbers make up a fifth of the population of Sarawak. Throughout the vast island of Borneo there are almost a quarter of a million of them. Of all the native peoples of the island, the Iban are thought to be among the late comers, being the first wave of true Malays. They are ultimately of

(Left) Even though some canoes now have outboard motors, rapids have to be crossed in the old way, by man power.

Iban women rarely leave their village. They do most of the farming while men are away, often for months, on trading trips to the coast.

Rivers like the Kasau are the only pathways through the dense jungle to the interior, and dugouts the normal method of transport.

Carefully balancing in the bows of a dugout, a fisherman skilfully casts a net. Fish are usually dried and eaten on feast days.

mongoloid stock and it seems likely that they came to the island by way of Sumatra. Today they live in the hills and on the lower and middle river courses of Sarawak. They are farmers and hunters, and because of their frequent forays to the coast, now mostly to trade, they are often known as the Sea Dayaks. In the recent past, the Iban were infamous as headhunters. This practice rested on an elaborate belief in a substance of the soul, possessed by all things. A man alive or dead possessed a soul; his hair, his teeth and his nails possessed one; beasts, trees, rice, stones, weapons, houses and boats all possessed souls. And the heads of slain enemies or murdered strangers ensured health and bountiful crops.

Past the sleepy white town of Kapit, where the Iban have come to trade their rubber, sago and rice with Chinese merchants, and where a score of Iban dugouts are moored by the river banks, the Rajang winds through the ever closer forest. Sometimes the sun vanishes behind black clouds and the air fills with rain. Those who have been caught in the torrent scramble from their boats into the river and help the craft against the current. All around the forest resounds to the cries of monkeys and hornbills and the rattle of insects.

Two days' travel from Kapit, the Iban long house of Rumah Ungka emerges from the forest beside the river. It is only a small long house, no more than 450 feet long. Between 200 and 300 people live beneath its roof. There are 50 separate rooms or *bilek,* each owned by a different family. The split-bamboo floor is covered with straw mats. Pages from Chinese and Malay color magazines

When this Iban woman has finished cooking a meal of rice, ferns and leaves she must serve the men first before she can eat.

are pinned to the flimsy partition walls. Huge earthenware jars filled with *tuak,* their own brew of rice alcohol, line a wall in every room. A few families boast a bed, though only for the father and mother; children sleep on long narrow mats which they roll up at daybreak.

The long house has an open terrace along one side and between this and the *bileks*, there is a long corridor. The corridor in front of each *bilek* is owned by the family, and called the *ruai*. At the time of the New Year it is filled with the Iban families who celebrate with feasting and *tuak* drinking. But before any glass is filled, a drop is spilled onto the floor – for the spirits of the long house. In the *ruai* on other days, women pound the rice in wooden mortars and the men hold important meetings. Drums, gongs and other ceremonial instruments hang from the walls and rafters. Traps and paddles from the dugout boats lean against the walls and near the entrance is the place where the smoke-blackened heads are attached to a circular frame. Beneath this frame there is a hearth where a fire is burned on ritual occasions and to keep the spirits of the heads warm.

The whole long house is raised some ten or twelve feet above the ground. Beneath it are stored boats not in use and all kinds of implements. There are pig-sties in the shade and protection underneath. The Iban are not clannish. They owe no particular allegiance to their homes in the long house and they move from one to another at will. The long house chief, or *Tua Rumah,* raises no objection. He has only limited authority over his people and his duties are confined to settling such matters as divorce cases. At Rumah Ungka, the Iban are easygoing; there are few disputes.

It was many years before the British administrators of the young colony of Sarawak were able to stamp out headhunting among the Iban and the neighboring Dayak tribes. Dr A C Haddon, an English anthropologist, commented at the turn of the century 'Headhunting is rigorously put down (in Sarawak), and rightly so; but when the government organizes a punitive expedition, say, to punish a recalcitrant headhunting chief, the natives comprising the government force are always allowed to keep what heads they can secure. Forty years later the government had taken a different line and opened up a new business. The officers kept a small store of human heads which they rented out to tribes for ceremonial purposes. A suitable fee was charged, and the number of the head and the date of the loan was recorded in a catalogue.

The wars between tribes in the forest are now over. The war canoes, once owned by every long house and which could carry as many as 50 men, are also gone. Instead the forest people live by farming, hunting and

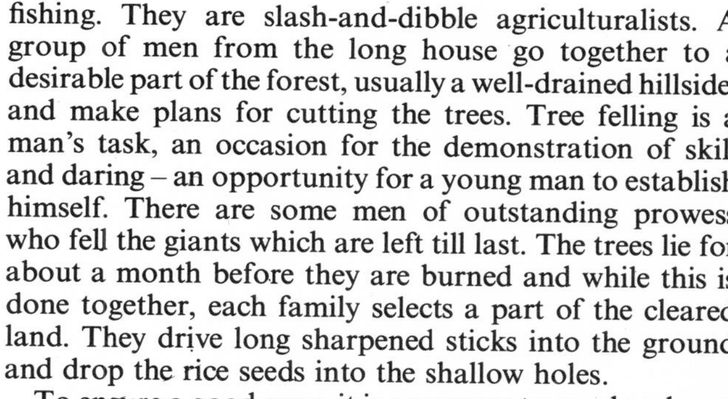

A village of over 200 people lives in each long house. Every family has its own room or *bilek* opening onto a common veranda.

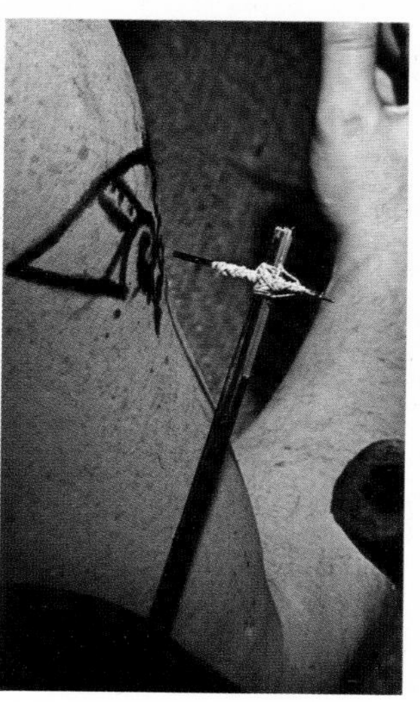

(Bottom) The tattooist uses a needle bound to a stick with white thread. After each session he polishes his client's skin with coconut oil.

fishing. They are slash-and-dibble agriculturalists. A group of men from the long house go together to a desirable part of the forest, usually a well-drained hillside, and make plans for cutting the trees. Tree felling is a man's task, an occasion for the demonstration of skill and daring – an opportunity for a young man to establish himself. There are some men of outstanding prowess who fell the giants which are left till last. The trees lie for about a month before they are burned and while this is done together, each family selects a part of the cleared land. They drive long sharpened sticks into the ground and drop the rice seeds into the shallow holes.

To ensure a good crop, it is necessary to weed and care for the growing plants. It is also essential to perform the religious and magical rituals which propitiate the spirits. Often many people – especially women – cluster about the clearings to perform these rituals from the time the young shoots appear until the harvest. When the time for reaping comes, women cut the first grain – containing the soul of the rice – with a crescent shaped blade. Harvest festivals and drinking and dancing accompany the storing of the grain in granaries.

After one year's cultivation, the cleared field is allowed to lie fallow until a growth of young trees has appeared. These are then cut and burned to replenish the soil in preparation for a second rice crop. This may be repeated three or four times, and then other crops – like yams, sugar cane and tobacco – are put in for one or two seasons. Within ten or fifteen years all the land in the vicinity of the long house has become exhausted. And then the long house is moved, or a smaller settlement is made in virgin forest and families live there for part of the year.

Early in the morning the women go to the river to bathe and to collect water for the long house. Soon they are preparing a meal for the family, and only eat when the men have finished. Then they are off to the fields and plots, or to search in the forest for roots and fruit. Later they pound and winnow the rice, preparing bowls with dried fish, dried bananas and eggs. The bowls are then laid in rows along the corridor as offerings to Pulangana, the god of peace. Some women are at work making baskets and mats. They are busy until evening, when they sit about to smoke and gossip or play with the children.

Hunting parties of men from the long house were, in the past, away in the forest for many days. While on the trip they gathered all kinds of fruit from the forest, or if they found caves, they collected edible birds' nests to trade with the Chinese. They caught pigs and deer in spring traps, in nooses and nets, but they depended mainly on blowguns and poisoned darts. These weapons were also used in their expeditions for enemy heads, but the fighting knives and bamboo spikes, which were planted in pits to cover a retreat, were the real weapons of war.

Before any raid the omens were consulted and only if everything was favorable would they set out in their war

Human heads, although no longer hunted, are used in rituals and are carried, carefully wrapped in leaves, to the ceremonial ground.

canoes. Strict taboos governed every act of the warriors. They wore close fitting rattan caps with hornbill feathers, and capes made of skin. They also carried long shields.

The warriors made their attack at dawn. If possible they simultaneously set the enemy long house on fire. Then, as the sleep-dazed inhabitants rushed out, they were killed or captured to be taken back as slaves. The war party heralded its return by singing in chorus, and just beyond their own long house they built a small hut in which the heads of their enemies were stored. For one night they camped out in the open. Then they decorated a bamboo pole with strips of palm leaf and set it up beside the figure of the war god. One of the fresh heads was set up beside the pole and boys approaching puberty were allowed to strike the skull. Women who had been captured were sometimes unfortunate if the Iban were building a new long house, for a girl had to be placed in the foundations. She was then crushed to death by the descent of the main house pillar.

Today hunting, like war between tribes, is on the wane. Trading expeditions have, for the Iban, replaced many of the hunting trips. And trade depends on the goods they have to sell – their agricultural produce. So subsistence still depends on grain cultivation, and on the timeliness and abundance of rainfall. Rituals are therefore important for, and geared to, the agricultural cycle. The New Year celebrations among the Iban are just such a ritual.

The womenfolk are busy all day in the long house preparing the food. Everyone is given an empty plate, in the center of which is placed the rice. This is then ringed with other foods. Suddenly the *Tua Rumah,* the long house chief, plucks three feathers from a chicken's wing, pricks the bird in the mouth and lets the blood drip into three glasses which already contain a little water. He stealthily spills the potion to propitiate the god of war, who might otherwise feel slighted and wreak revenge. After this ceremony, offerings are laid in a decorated wooden vessel and hoisted to a beam of the communal room. Later everyone dines on wild boar and deer cooked on bamboo sticks over a fire. It is a special day for the Iban. Normally they eat only cooked ferns and leaves with their rice. Soon the dancing begins, and everyone becomes exhilarated by the occasion and the effects of the *tuak*.

The men of the long house begin to run in many directions with reluctant chickens under their arms. The *tuak* runs freely. And then the *Tua Rumah* appears again, but this time to dance. He is dressed in a long white goatskin poncho, a wrap around loin-cloth made of bright silk, a sword in a silver-inlaid sheath and a rattan cap stuck with huge feathers. He dances with the others to the rhythm of gongs struck by the children. He stretches out his long arms which are covered in tattoos, he closes his eyes and bends slowly, twisting his feet and pivoting on his knees. His arms sway like the wings of a wounded bird. He crouches, then springs high, whirling and then landing in his crouching position. In the old

The New Year is celebrated with feasting but first a drop of *tuak*, rice wine, is spilled on the floor for the spirits of the long house.

days, the chief and the menfolk would dance all night before setting out on a headhunting expedition. Sometimes the motive was vengeance, for the killing of one of their fellow tribesmen. But the heads they brought back would also bring great prestige to them. It was not difficult then to find a wife.

Now the men dance until they collapse. In the morning they are still sprawled where they fell the night before. The young girls and women go to the river to bathe. They sit on logs floating on the water and comb their hair. As they chatter and laugh, some reveal gold-plated teeth; a few have tiny green or red hearts painted on them.

A little further upstream from Rumah Ungka, there is the long house of Sanda Rumah. It is an even larger long house. In its vast corridor, in the many *ruai*, hang rattan cages which house dusty human skulls. They are sinister reminders of the past, symbols of Iban ferocity. The heads belonged to Japanese soldiers killed during World War II. It was the last time the Iban had demonstrated their traditional ferocity.

At the time of the festival of long life, here too there is celebration and dancing. The long house chief dances in a circle about a bamboo pole. He stamps the ground with a stick adorned with feathers and bells. He addresses ritual sayings to the gods of long life. His voice is gentle, but he has sharp eyes. As night falls, all the tribesmen chant songs and verses. They sound like incantations in a cathedral. Then afterwards, in the early mist of dawn, the men disappear into the forest. They carry spears and swords as though they were going to hunt heads. But they are only after wild boar and deer.

There is a long house tattooist at Sanda Rumah. At the end of each session he polishes his client's skin with coconut oil. One man has his back, his legs, his arms and neck all covered in intricate designs of flowers and arabesques. The tattooist uses a needle bound to a stick with white thread. The needle is dipped in black dye. It is an ancient art among the Iban, though it does not flourish as it did. A man would always be tattooed, not only for the beauty of the designs, but also to protect him from wildcats who would mistake him for one of their own kind. It is said now that only the bravest of men have their hands tattoed, for you can read from their hands how many heads they have cut.

In Sarawak the government attempts to draw the Iban into the 20th century. Since they have such a large population, they have been given political representation in the parliament. Their chief is the Minister for Sarawak Affairs. He has long, flowing hair which he refuses to cut; he also refuses to wear a coat and tie except when he leaves his people's country. Once, in the parliament, he was insulted in the course of a speech by an opposition member. The Iban chief replied courteously in his own language, inviting the man to come to Iban country. 'My people' he said 'will show you how we cut off men's heads and hang them in our homes as decoration.'

Toradja
Sulwasi (Celebes)

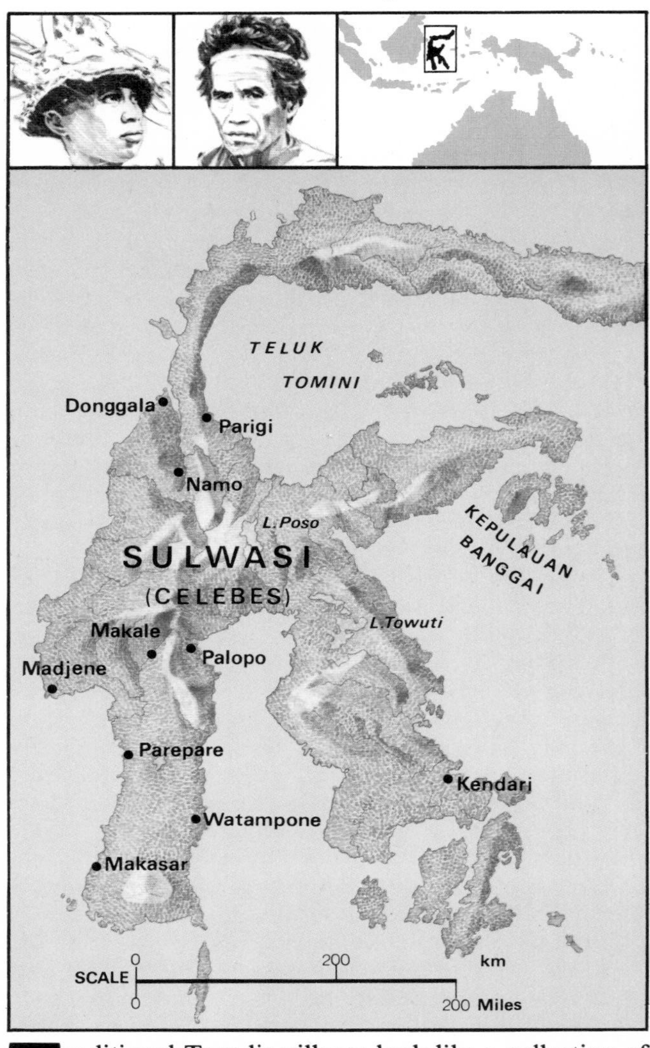

Traditional Toradja villages look like a collection of arks floating in a sea of green tropical vegetation. Their tall narrow houses built on piles have bamboo or palm wood floors, plaited walls and thatched eaves which curve out back and front like the prow and stern of a ship. These roofs of split bamboo, with interlocking flat strips of pounded bamboo, keep the house warm and also act as protection against the torrential rains. The Toradja decorate the outside of their houses with carved panels which they paint with black, white, orange and yellow traditional designs. Sometimes they put a carved wooden water buffalo head or buffalo horns on the front of their houses as well. Buffalo are the Toradja's sign of wealth – they evaluate them according to their color. They rate piebald ones highest – these are worth nearly twenty times the price of an ordinary black animal.

The Toradja are the highlanders who live in the mountainous interior regions of the central part of the island of Sulwasi (formerly Sulawesi or Celebes) in Indonesia.

Tau-tau, wooden effigies of generations of Toradja dead, stand outside family crypts. They are erected at the end of rites which may last years.

There are a number of Toradja peoples, among them the eastern group, the twenty tribes of Bare'e speaking Toradja, who live around and to the north, south and east of Lake Poso in the center of the island. In the past, when the tribes were hostile to each other, they nevertheless recognized a higher authority in the ruler of one or another of a number of coastal kingdoms, particularly Luwu and Mori. Today the tribes are not hostile, but bound together by a sense of common origin and kinship. And they have no overall ruler, but live in a number of independent villages over a well-defined area.

Toradja houses are each occupied by several families. Inside they are sparsely furnished with only a few rough benches and a table but no beds. The Toradja prefer to sleep on the floor on woven reed mats and wrapped up in their sarongs. They cook their food on an open fire. And near the houses will be a larger number of barns – one for each family – where they keep their rice.

Life in the villages is communal, but with social divisions based on sex, age and class. Every Toradja has a hereditary rank: the highest are nobles and the lowest servants. Once the servant class were slaves, but although completely under the control of their masters they were never exploited mercilessly and were often greatly respected by the families that owned them. It was the other slaves – whom the Toradja had bought or captured in battle – that they frequently used as their human sacrifices.

Each Toradja family today owns a few domestic animals such as water buffalo and pigs and also a supply of cotton goods. Each year the family heads with the village chief and elders decide which families should cultivate which tracts of land. A family can only maintain its right to their allocation of land by keeping it under constant cultivation. The extended families, of which each family is a part, own herds of buffalo, sago palms and bamboo groves which are shared equally by all members. The male head of the extended family usually controls the family property, although this duty is sometimes taken over by the senior female. Nothing can be sold without the consent of all. Family groups which try to keep their property to themselves are frowned on, for in Toradja society it is believed that all possessions should be shared by all members of the community. The Toradja consider generosity a great virtue. Richer families are particularly respected if they make generous contributions to religious festivals.

The Toradja hold old age in great respect and political affairs are governed by the elders and the village chief. The entire village selects for its chief the man they feel has the most suitable qualities. He must have the courage to protect the village from demands on its people or property. He must be a skilful enough orator to win legal disputes and be willing and able to help his fellow villagers in need. And he must, which is perhaps most important, have a thorough knowledge of the traditions of his society, the

Toradja life is based on the interaction of opposites: life, daytime, good, masculinity against death, night-time, evil and femininity.

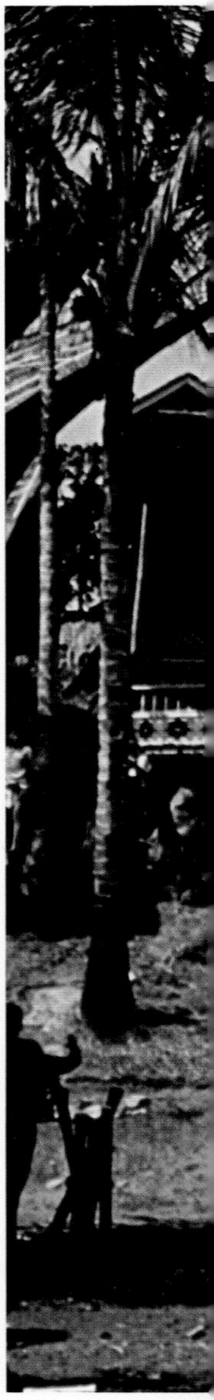

Villagers and guests gather for the funeral rites of a chief whose corpse has lain for months, swathed in quilts, in his high-roofed house.

The warriors' dance is performed at the funeral, a relic of Toradja headhunting times. A dancer wears a necklace of human rib bones.

A fisherman climbs up to his rickety bamboo platform in the Celebes Sea; he will sit there all night long waiting for a catch.

talent to organize the various village activities and the ability to make and take decisions for his followers. He has no official power to enforce any of his decisions. His authority depends entirely on the vital support of his ancestors and his success depends on his ability to reconcile the conflicting interests of his villagers. To succeed he must try to lead the village elders in discussion and persuade them that what he thinks is right for the community. If a chief tries to behave in an autocratic manner his fellow villagers simply withdraw their loyalty and leave him to rule only his own family. And although a chief's authority does not extend outside his own village he acts as its representative in his dealings with other villages.

All the Toradja's activities are in a sense directed towards maintaining a way of life which they believe their ancestors bequeathed them. They believe that everything results from the interaction of opposites. The universe itself is bi-polar with an upperworld and an underworld, inhabited by opposing forces and supernatural beings, with the Toradja's real world in between. The upperworld is mainly associated with daytime, life, good and masculinity, but it also contains gods and spirits of night-time: death, evil and female. The underworld, likewise, though associated with night-time, death, evil and femininity also contains gods and spirits representing their opposites. There are two other gods, 'Man' who lives in the upperworld, and 'Maid' who lives in the underworld. And there is the principal god who they believe created them and who punishes them for major sins. This supreme god lives in the upperworld, but he too has an evil opposite, called 'the Night', who lives in the underworld. The guardian spirits of the Toradja shamans live in the upperworld but have there numerous enemies in the form of evil spirits. The Toradja always associate their dead with the underworld but yet believe them to have both an evil and beneficent aspect. They also think of the jungle as evil and the village as good although again they believe that their world is inhabited by both good and bad spirits, and that there are evil people in human society – witches and sorcerers – as well as good people.

At the beginning of the 20th century, when the Toradja were visited and first intensively studied by Dutch missionaries, their society included a number of specialists who dealt with the supernatural. The basic division of labor in the supernatural area was on a sexual basis. All adult males, for example, were headhunters whose duty it was to their ancestors to kill their enemies continuously and regularly. If one assumes, as they did, that life is simply the opposite of death then it is easy to understand why they thought that one cannot exist without the other. The Toradja believed that the health and fertility of the people and their crops depended on the taking of heads. The headhunters were supported by a group of ancestors who lived in village temples which

Water buffalo are workers in the *padi* fields and an important source of wealth, their stylized images are painted on house fronts.

Everyone joins in a funeral. The splendour of the ceremony and the number of buffalo slaughtered testifies to the dead man's importance.

were decorated with explicitly sexual symbols. While men were associated with death and ancestors, Toradja women dealt with the living, supported by spirits in the upperworld. Women acted as shamans whose primary duties were to fetch the souls of newborn babies from the upperworld and to retrieve the souls of sick people from whatever part of the universe to which they might have strayed. They did this by sending out their own souls at night to other worlds. Totally enclosed in a special tent they described, in a sacred language, their voyages to the other worlds in long poetic litanies.

Today the Toradja still believe that each person has two souls: a death soul, that sees that he reaches his preordained end, and a life soul, that makes up both his life essence and particular personality. When a Toradja dies the life soul disappears and a new death soul comes into being.

The Toradja have many rituals, but those connected with death and with the cultivation of rice are most important. They treat rice as a human being. The soul of rice too is fetched from the upperworld. During the rice festival the Toradja dance and sing throughout the night, re-enacting the rice growing cycle from planting to harvesting. At some point during the festivities the ancestors and all the gods and spirits of the universe are invoked.

The other great ritual for the Toradja is connected with death. In line, again, with their theory of opposites, they believe that the dead do everything the opposite way to the living. They walk, but upside-down. They talk the Toradja language, but backwards. And their crops succeed when those of the living fail. Although living Toradja rely on the support of their dead in everything they do, they also fear the mischief that the spirits might be tempted to perform.

When a Toradja chief dies his body is wrapped in homespun quilting and laid in a darkened room upstairs in his house. The shutters are closed and festooned outside with *krises* – ancestral daggers which are among the Toradja's most treasured heirlooms. Here the dead chief lies with his head pointing towards the west, and his bowl and cup by his side, as if to imply he is only ill. For several months the body lies there drying in its absorbent chrysalis until it is time for the first of the funeral rites.

Before the funeral the villagers build a series of temporary bamboo buildings around the chief's house where the funeral guests will stay. The guests start to arrive. They stream along the road to the village, bringing gifts for the dead chief. Some carry chickens in baskets; some, pigs strung up on bamboo poles, and others bundles of rice and bamboo tubes of *tuak* – a frothy, mildly intoxicating drink that the Toradja make from sugar palm oil. When the visitors arrive they are greeted by a village official who leads them past two men seated at a table who record the gifts that are presented.

For centuries the Toradja have maintained a network of debts which are usually paid back at funerals. By keeping a careful record the village officials know which debts have been paid and note down any new ones as they are incurred.

When all the guests have arrived and the gifts are all recorded the funeral ceremony begins. After a period of ritual singing and dancing everybody goes to the chief's house and the body is brought out. To wild cries it is tossed in the air and caught several times and then laid gently on the ground with the feet pointing towards the south, indicating that the chief is finally dead. His body is returned to his house where it lies attended by his wife. The funeral ceremony continues for several days with singing, dancing and feasting. The songs and dancing mourn the dead chief but, true to Toradja religious belief, they are at the same time celebrating the continuance of life. Formerly, before Dutch missionaries put a stop to it at the beginning of the 20th century, funerals were an occasion for the Toradja to sacrifice their buffalo. Some of these buffalo would have been given in payment for old debts and others contributed by

Guests display live pigs slung from bamboo poles which they have brought to the funeral to repay the dead man's past generosity.

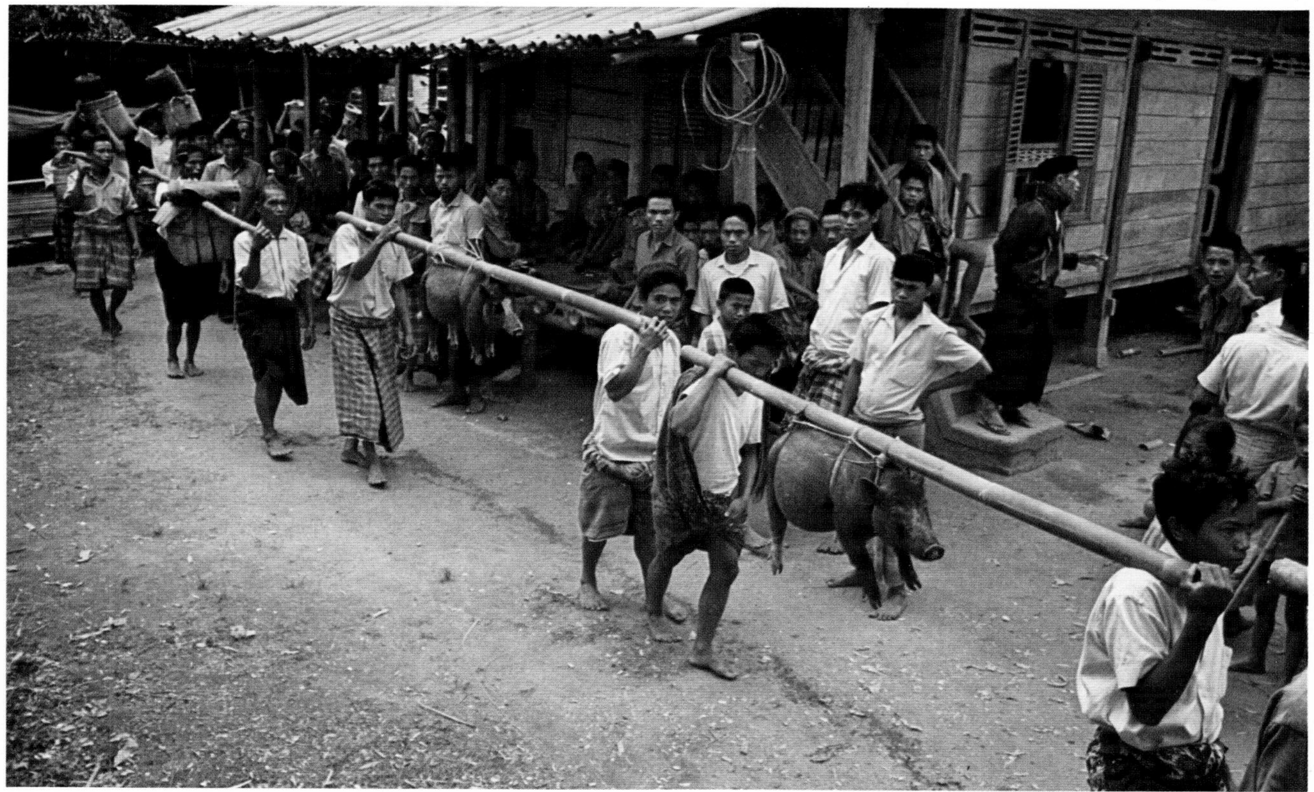

the villagers. Their meat was eaten and distributed among guests and relatives of the dead person. Today although they no longer sacrifice their buffalo some Toradja groups do stage buffalo fights at funeral spectacles which they very much enjoy.

When the celebrations are over the guests take their leave and return to their own villages. Still the body of the chief has not been finally buried – the final funeral takes place months, sometimes even a year later. Placed in a boat-shaped coffin the body is borne from the village to one of the surrounding cliff faces and placed high up in a tomb chiseled out from the rock. The door is sealed and human effigies are placed on the ledge outside. The effigies, dressed in Toradja clothes and with recognizable human faces stare down like real people. Outside the chief's tomb the effigies will often have eyes of gold. Here in his tomb – the Toradja believe – their chief finally returns to the bosom of his ancestors.

Although all Toradja know and believe in a creator god, their ancestors still seem more important to them. The Toradja who have been converted to Islam place Allah in the underworld as the ruler of Maka (Mecca) the city of the dead. And Toradja villages which have been converted to Christianity hold a final funeral for the bones of their dead in which they inform their ancestors that they can no longer adhere to the old customs because they are about to follow a 'new road'.

Singing, dancing and feasting will continue for several days, not only to mourn the dead man but to celebrate the continuation of life.

Javanese villagers
Indonesia

Every grain of rice from the *padi* fields is precious to the Javanese who have one of the most dense populations in the world.

The island of Java is a chain of over 100 volcanic mountains, 35 of them still active. High rugged plateaux cover much of the interior of the eastern and western parts of the island. But in the middle the line of the plateau breaks, and broad valleys lie between Mount Merapi in the west to Mount Kelud in the east. These gentle sloping interior valleys of central Java are well drained and exceptionally fertile. Since the 5th century AD they have been superbly shaped into an irrigated agricultural landscape that has steadily supported one of the most dense populations of the world.

Javanese peasants live and work all over the varied terrain of the island – on the flat plains or the sides of steep volcanoes – in villages set among vegetable plots, tobacco fields, orchard plantations and irrigated rice fields. The villages are nearly invisible, buried in the deep layers of vegetation which cover the island – green coconut palms, high crowned fruit trees, banana palms and bamboo. Only the squared-off edges of the greenery, the thoroughly cultivated fields in between, and the dirt roads and irrigation canals that run across the fields in straight lines and at right angles as far as the terrain permits, suggest the intensity of the villagers' work.

The houses are tucked neatly into the greenery that surrounds them. With walls of sturdily woven bamboo or soft baked clay and roof tiles of red-brown clay they are rectangular and stand neatly aligned with the roads. Houses vary widely in size but they are all of the same architectural design: the smallest are eight by ten feet, the largest, built by placing two or three rectangular units side by side, are 40 by 50 feet.

The standard architectural design of the basic rectangular, gable-roofed unit allows villagers to build houses the size they want. The building is done by a traditionally skilled village carpenter helped by a work party of neighbors. The units are all interchangeable and villagers carry on a lively trade in used house parts: growing families buy units to improve their houses, and other families trade in more valuable pieces for cheaper ones when they are short of cash.

Inside the front room there is always a table and four chairs (or the nearest thing to it that a family can afford) set square in the center of the room. The table and chairs stand as a sign that the family can afford to receive guests, and thus have the right to be asked in return to other families. When guests arrive their host and his wife sit down with them at the table and talk politely. Eventually the guests are served with tea or coffee and some simple food after which they are expected to leave. There is no common dining area because each person ordinarily eats alone at his own time; there are no family meals. If the house is large there will be other dimly lit rooms filled with wardrobes, bits of treasured bric-à-brac and other possessions. Behind these rooms are the sleeping cubicles: one for the husband and wife (plus one child), one for daughters, and sometimes one

(Left) Most of the rice crop is sold and villagers eat substitutes like maize and cassava, with only small amounts of rice mixed in.

for sons, although boys often sleep in small groups in one another's front rooms or in the village guard sheds.

Attached to the rear of one side of the house is an enclosed cooking area, with a simple brick open-hearth stove using wood or charcoal and with large storage jars, plain blackened pots and pans, and stores of loose garden produce hanging from the roof. The floors, except in well-to-do houses, are of earth, packed hard and smooth. The front room and in front of the house are public; the back and behind the house are for privacy and intimacy, where the women and children are more often to be found, and adults gather to chat at night.

Families of husband, wife and children tend to live alone, but they sometimes take in grandparents or young unmarried brothers and sisters and occasionally more distant young or elderly relatives who are in need. Fathers are very often step-fathers, as the divorce rate among the Javanese is exceptionally high (in the rural area where I worked there was one divorce for every two marriages registered). Divorced women with children find it easy to remarry, although some choose not to and are happy to live without a man around the house.

Every Javanese villager's life is centered around farming. Rice is cultivated everywhere in the island, but where the climate is favorable farmers also grow other crops. In eastern Java during the dry season from June to October the farmers grow soyabeans, corn, peanuts, onions, cassava, tobacco and various vegetables. But in western Java, which has a more regular rainfall throughout the year, the farmers concentrate on cultivating a double crop of rice. And in the cooler highlands of both east and west Java they can grow European vegetables, coffee, tea and pineapples. But rice remains the staple crop and food.

The villagers value rice very highly as a food. I spoke to a man about it once and he insisted that a large piece of steak would be no substitute in his stomach for rice. In fact most villagers can only afford rice for a short time each year for they sell off all they produce. They eat in its place cheaper substitutes, such as corn and cassava, mixed up with small amounts of rice to make the meal more palatable. The daily ration for one adult is reckoned at one pound of uncooked rice, or its equivalent in a substitute. Although rice or a substitute is the basis of any proper meal the villagers flavor it by adding very hot chili peppers, considered essential to good health, and soyabean curd or cake. The villagers do not eat meat – chicken, goat, mutton, water buffalo or beef – except on special occasions.

A family derives its social independence from its ability to feed not only itself, but also guests when they visit. Only when a couple can do this are they recognized by the community as an independent unit able, as is required of them, to participate in village affairs, to invite and be invited to other family celebrations, and to negotiate for loans and land concessions of their own.

Villagers near Bandung on the wetter western side of Java harvest two rice crops each year. In the east other crops are grown in the dry season.

(Bottom) The growing rice must be kept submerged in water brought up from a nearby canal by a simple but efficient treadmill.

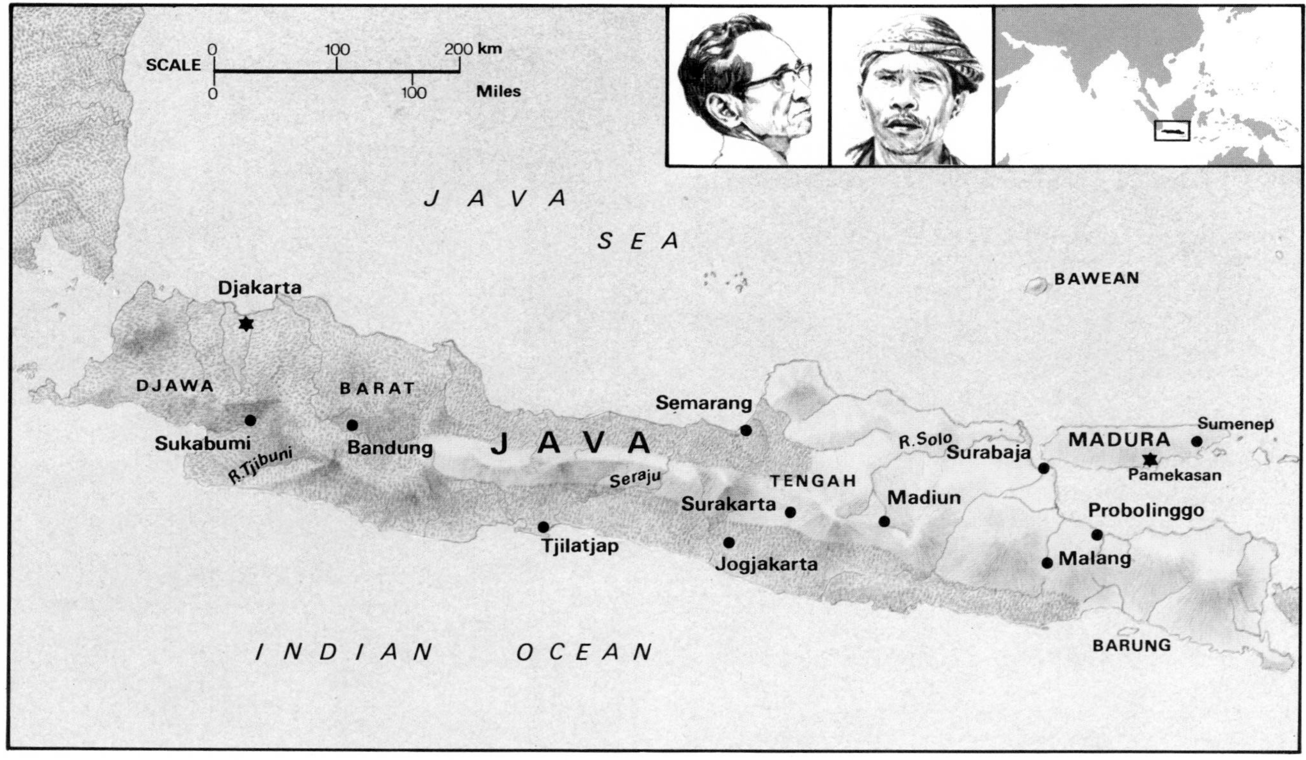

And it is this independence, the very foundation of Java society, that is now being threatened. All over Java the enormous numbers of villagers who are trying to make a livelihood from farming cause a drastic land shortage.

At least 75 million people (in 1972) live on the island of Java which (including the island of Madura off Java's north-east coast) covers an area of 51,000 square miles. And 75 per cent of this population is rural. The remainder are heavily bureaucratic and mercantile rather than industrially productive. These figures reveal the major problems of life for the Javanese villager. The pressures upon rural life are unbelievably high. I lived and worked in a relatively prosperous farming area in east Java where nearly 96 per cent of the villagers depended directly upon farming for a livelihood and the population density was 2,200 people per square mile. In some rural areas it exceeds 5,000 people per square mile.

The sheer quantity of people on the Javanese rural scene can only be grasped when it is likened not to the rural countryside of the west, with isolated farms, or small villages separated from each other by miles of fields and woods, but to moderately dense suburban clusters, either adjoining each other or separated by a few hundred yards at most. Within these clusters, the houses are tightly packed, and getting more so every year. In the village where I lived in 1953 and 1954 more than 1,500 people occupy some three hundred houses in a residential area of about one-fifth of a square mile. The residential area on two sides of the village extended beyond its boundaries, unbroken for miles. The older villagers reckoned that the population had increased four-fold over the preceding fifty years, and I do not think the expansion has slowed down during the nearly twenty years since my stay.

Village life pulsates with people. From birth a Javanese baby is quite literally surrounded with them. For five days and nights after the birth the mother and child are constantly surrounded by a protective swarm of people – women by day and men by night – who come from all over the village and often beyond to keep the vigil. Children grow up continually carried or attended, not only by their mother, but by their father, kinsmen, brothers and sisters, and close neighbors who play with them and mother them. Girls start early on domestic chores, which they do in a group with sisters and visiting relatives and neighbors. Boys join their friends to work at each other's farm plots and by night roam in bands about the village and beyond looking for entertainment. And although married men will often work at some tasks alone or with just one or two relatives or neighbors on their land, planting, irrigating, harvesting, building or repairing houses, working on roads or dams for the village, the ceremonial preparations tend to be carried out by large work parties of men and women. At family celebrations, marriages and circumcisions the nights are filled with gong music and the villagers crowd together

A volcanic mountain dominates the main street of Temang-gung. It is dormant now, without power to threaten the busy human lives at its feet.

(Center) Cotton is spun by hand in a batik works in Djakarta where waxed cloth is dyed in intricate patterns using 2,000 year-old methods.

The dyeing process is complete and the wax is removed from the cloth by ironing over a sheet of paper which will absorb the melted wax.

Bull-racing championships are held regularly at Pamekasan on the island of Madura where the best Javanese cattle are raised.

by the hundreds in the families' yards to watch shadow puppet shows or live dance dramas till dawn. And when a villager dies neighbors and kinsmen immediately down their tools and crowd about the bereaved family, calming them, showering them with help and gifts of food and immediately setting up the funeral ceremony and burial at the village graveyard nearby.

The constant, gentle flow and presence of people is deeply comforting for most villagers. But paradoxically it is just the presence of all these people in the villages that creates the major pressure of village life – the scarcity of land.

More and more young villagers, whose families have been unable to give them any rights to land, are faced with limited and not very rewarding options. They can work for wages, planting, weeding and harvesting other crops than rice, but the work is scarce, seasonal and badly paid. Also families who are not well-to-do and need to hire labor often give work to people who they think can offer it in return to them some time.

Many young couples try to earn money from other sources. They buy food, cooked and uncooked, in the local town markets and sell it in the villages. They weave bamboo matting and work at other crafts. They hire themselves out as general haulers – as really no more than beasts of burden. The wages for these jobs are just about in line with daily wages for farm work. But even if a family can scrape together enough money to buy a sewing machine, a bicycle or some carpenter's tools all of which will greatly increase what they can earn, there is not enough steady employment to support a household without supplementary earnings. There are plenty of village families limited to these rather dead-end options particularly in the more densely populated areas, and where the terrain or lack of water prevent year-round agriculture.

What every couple hopes for is to gain some rights to farm land. Potentially, full rights can be bought, rented or acquired from the village stock of communal farm land. But communal rights in villages are, where they exist, in fact held almost entirely by a minority of senior families. There are virtually no shares available to the landless. Rents, let alone prices, are far beyond the reach of almost all landless families. The only solution for these people is sharecropping: But here too opportunities are not only scarce but only minimally rewarding. For sharecroppers receive varying, but invariably small, amounts of the crop depending on how much they contribute in labor and costs. The lowest concession a sharecropper can get is one-fifth to one-tenth of the crop in return for cultivating it (although the landlord pays the costs of plowing, harvesting, and seeding).

Worshippers leave Borobudur near Magelang, a square pyramid dating from the 8th century, the most elaborate Buddhist temple in the world.

Higher concessions give the sharecropper one-third of the crop in return for responsibility to plow, plant and cultivate it. The landlord provides the seed and each pays the cost of harvesting his share of the crop. The most rewarding concession gives the sharecropper half the crop in exchange for being totally responsible for cultivating it and sharing only the harvesting costs with the landlord.

The ideal for a landless couple is to work their way up by getting higher and higher concessions, eventually building capital in livestock, a plow and a cash reserve with which they can rent and perhaps even buy land outright. But there is not much room at the top. Concessions for half shares are increasingly rare, in spite of government regulations to the contrary. The available land is increasingly split up into smaller and smaller parcels of plots, sharecropping concessions, and wage work. Resources have been even further fragmented by the strong pressure in the villages towards sharing available agricultural production widely among people who have little or no direct access to land. This is done through extended use of traditional technology and labor and intensive cultivation, called 'shared poverty'.

All Javanese villages are not however equally poor. Distribution of land rights varies sharply from village to village – even between villages where all or a large part of the farmland is held communally. Inequality increases in the denser areas and near large cities when half to two-thirds or more of the population lack any direct rights to land. In my relatively prosperous area, two-fifths of the households held virtually no rights to farmland, while three or four households held what were, by village standards, very substantial lands. Even among those people who have land rights, there is a sharp social division between the people who have enough and do not need to work for wages or enter into dependent sharecropping relations with well-to-do households, and the people who can afford to avoid such demeaning sources of livelihood. Perhaps one-third to one-quarter of the people who had land rights in my rural area could demonstrate such independence.

The villagers can call on only limited help from the administration in their dilemma. Each village has a small staff of officials, elected by the villagers, who are at the bottom of the state system of territorial administration. Although they look after its irrigation system, its security and its communally held land they do not attempt to solve new problems, particularly the problems of lack of land and irrigation water, both acutely needed by the expanding population. And although the officials of amalgamated villages have more authority, even their powers are very limited. There are simply no official channels through which the villagers can realistically hope to solve their problems.

In 1963 groups of poorer villagers, especially in eastern Java began to try and solve their problems by themselves. They took advantage of the land reform legislation that had been passed a year or two earlier, which sharply limited the size of individual land holdings and the share a landlord could claim from a sharecropper. The villagers began to take over, and redistribute among themselves, parcels of land owned by large landlords, claiming that they were simply carrying out laws which their local officials were too frightened or indifferent to enforce. At the same time poorer sharecropping farmers began secretly withholding all or part of the shares they owed their landlords, especially from absentee urban landlords, many of them civil servants.

Also in 1963, in west Java, agricultural colleges began to send their students to live in villages to help the farmers intensify their agriculture at the same time as teaching students what farming was really like. This quickly showed promising results as the students, with their greater political sophistication and upper class urban contacts, were able to help farmers get the government supplies due to them through the sometimes obstructive local bureaucratic networks. The program, called BIMAS, was backed by the government and it was considerably expanded throughout 1964. In effect the students were helping the villagers to minimize their dependence on the local administrative and economic establishments.

But all this virtually ended in 1965, when a small band of left-wing and communist army officers, in the name of defending President Sukarno against a military coup, assassinated most of the top army leaders. The coup d'état failed and it triggered off a massive wave of slaughter throughout Indonesia of people locally identified as communist or 'leftist'. In Java the militant farmers became particular targets as their anti-landlord actions were greatly feared by the conservative and well-to-do landowners. The BIMAS program was badly crippled and the students withdrawn from the villages.

The new government that has taken over since the assassinations has taken strong measures to solve the villagers' problems. They send technical experts to the villagers to advise on needed changes. They have made contracts with foreign agronomic corporations to put massive doses of capital and know-how into Javanese farming. This technological program of agricultural reform was called the 'green revolution'.

But the new program has up till now been disappointing. The credits and supplies have been cheerfully accepted by individual farmers, but so far this priming has not produced any substantial flow back into the national economy. One main problem seems to be that the administrators are reluctant to give any real political power to the village communities, for such a redistribution would mean conflict, which the present government is most anxious to avoid. As a result the 'green revolution' to date has not shown great promise as a solution to rural Java's acute problems.

A backstage view of a puppet show. The *dalang* holds up his puppets before entranced villagers while behind him sit a singer and musicians.

The god-like figure of Rama, hero of the Hindu epic poem Ramayana, is a popular character in the shadow plays performed all over Indonesia.

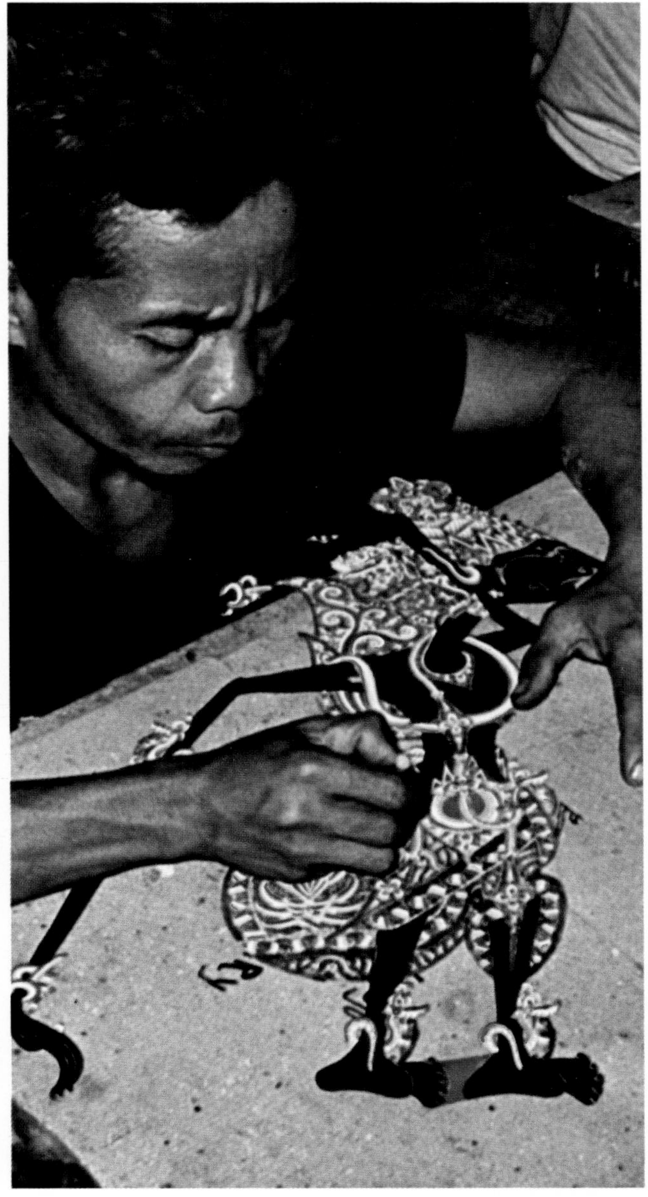

Shadow puppets are carved out of leather and then richly painted and gilded by the puppet maker, a highly skilled craftsman.

Balinese
Indonesia

The island of Bali is extravagantly beautiful. Massive active volcanoes rise from the center, reaching 10,000 feet, and mysteriously cloaked in clouds. Sunk in the mountain heights are the smooth turquoise gems of volcanic lakes. Down the mountain slopes runs a mosaic of bright green terraced ricefields, interrupted by villages and temples among clumps of trees, and reaching down towards coconut groves, white beaches and a startlingly blue sea.

But despite Bali's beauty, and the strength of its distinctive culture, it has not been and is not peaceful and serene. In this century Bali has been conquered by the Dutch and by the Japanese. Independence as part of the Republic of Indonesia brought traumatic changes, and an abortive coup in 1965 brought massacre. In 1917, 1926 and 1963 there were disastrous volcanic eruptions. Today the Balinese face problems of overpopulation: more than 2 million people live on the island, in an area of little more than 2,000 square miles. Land shortage is only slightly relieved by emigration. Tourism, which is increasingly important to the island's strained economy

Monkey men perform a modern dance based on a Hindu Ramayana tale of a princess rescued from the evil king of Lanka by an army of monkeys.

The main village street runs down a slope, from Balinese 'north' to 'south'. At the top is the 'origin temple', at the bottom, temples for the dead.

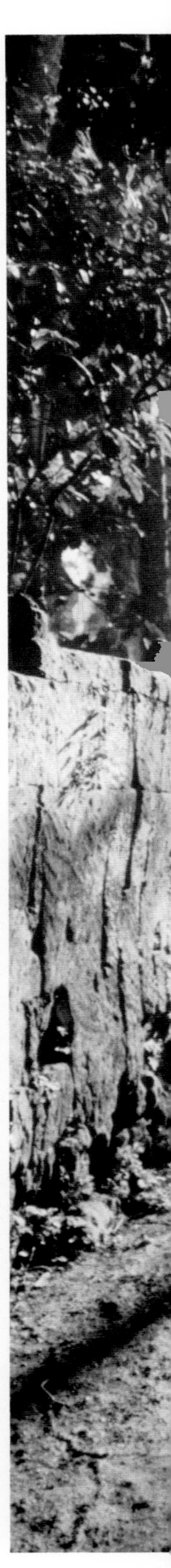

The Muderi family water their cattle at the village spring. People bathe and drink in the outer troughs; cattle use the middle one.

Balinese villagers are staunchly independent. Under five elected elders, all the men hold an equal place in the village assembly.

and which provides vital foreign currency, threatens the existence of the very culture which the tourists seek. Already the government is so worried about this danger that it is trying to confine the tourists' activities to the south-east of the island. Yet despite these threats a living culture does survive. It centers on a strong living religion.

The ancient, indigenous culture of the island to which Hindu elements attached themselves increasingly from the 2nd century AD remained the core of modern Balinese culture. This was strengthened by influences from the 11th century onwards of contacts with the Hindu-ized courts of Java, which culminated in the conquest of Bali in 1334 by the great Majapahit empire of East Java. The Javanese-Hindu period on Bali began. Within 400 years there developed a hybrid Balinese civilization, the product of enrichment by the talents of the priests, scholars, scribes, artists, musicians, dancers and craftsmen of the Majapahit court. It was a civilization full of variety, from the courts, where much of the Javanese culture had been maintained, to isolated mountain villages where the indigenous Balinese, the Bali Aga, retained many of their ancient ways. It was nevertheless a unified civilization, and its strength lay in the Bali-Hindu culture of south central Bali, where the large villages were able to support many arts even when the courts declined after Dutch conquest in 1908.

The religion at the heart of this civilization is based on ancestor worship and spirit cults combined with Javanese Hinduism. It is maintained by independent local communities who worship the sun, earth and water as the sources of life, and mountains, from which rivers flow, as the sources of fertility. Sacred Gunung Agung, the highest mountain, is the focus of ritual, center of the universe and home of Siwa the supreme deity. On its south-west slope is the temple of Pura Besakih where offerings are made for the well-being of the whole nation. In this mountain world live the gods and the spirits of the ancestors. At the other pole is the sea and the underworld, the abode of devils, demons and evil spirits. Everyday life is influenced by the spirit activity of both worlds and it is necessary to balance both these forces, pleasing the protective powers and placating the evil by rituals, offerings and sacrifices. These ceremonies can only be effective if the performers are spiritually pure. Polluting acts, association with blood, sickness or death must be avoided and cleanliness ensured by preparatory rituals. More thoroughly perhaps than in any other country religion is lived in Bali, from the mighty Pura Besakih to the small shrines tended in every home and in the 20,000 temples throughout the island.

The Balinese believe in, and possess, an ordered world in which everyone knows his place symbolically – in the opposition of good to evil, gods to demons, mountains to sea, and literally—in the positioning of people during ceremonies and in the orientation of buildings which always have the most sacred part nearest to the moun-

Much of the Balinese coast is steep and rocky, but there are some small fishing villages like Kuta where men fish by night from canoes.

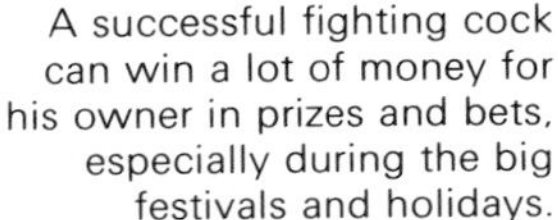

A successful fighting cock can win a lot of money for his owner in prizes and bets, especially during the big festivals and holidays.

tains. This demands a strong sense of community and a constant effort towards well ordered behavior.

Part of this order is imposed socially by hereditary titles or *wangsa* which rank everyone from birth. The mass of the people fall into the lowest of four ranks, the Jaba. Perhaps ten per cent bear *triwangsa* titles, similar to the three highest Hindu castes – Brahmana, Satria and Vesia. The *triwangsa* take more precautions against pollution than Jaba and only they can become *pedanda,* high priests, who perform the most sacred rituals. Otherwise titles control prestige alone. Descendants of princely families command respect but retain little actual power. In etiquette, however, distinctions are always made, particularly in language.

There are three forms of Balinese language. Low Balinese is the everyday language for most people, but high Balinese must be used when addressing a person of higher rank. When there is doubt about relative status it is polite to use the third form, middle Balinese.

The local representatives of any title-group form patrilineal clans or *dadia,* whose members depend on each other for economic, political and religious assistance. Whenever possible, clans build their own temples for their own ancestors – an extension of household shrines where they make daily offerings of a flower, rice, some salt and chili, all wrapped in a banana leaf.

A man normally marries a girl from within his clan, and lives with his father until he can build or get a house of his own. Higher caste marriages tend to be arranged, but usually a man and a girl decide for themselves when they will marry. Sometimes a wedding begins spectacularly with a pre-arranged kidnapping of the girl, although a quiet elopement is more common. When the couple returns, a formal ceremony before a priest is followed by celebrations, feasting and entertainment. All Balinese are expected to marry, and until a man is married he cannot join the village association and take a responsible part in village affairs. Husband and wife form a team with clearly defined tasks. Men do all the agricultural work, with assistance from their wives and children at harvest

Contributions of rice are weighed for the irrigation tax. Several neighboring villages share the same irrigation system.

(Right) Terraces climb the steep hillsides near Pudjung where rich volcanic soil yields two crops of irrigated rice each year.

time. A man is also responsible for housebuilding and any heavy manual work. Women are responsible for bringing up the children and for household work. They also hold the purse strings and do most of the market trading.

Children are not only welcomed when they are born, but treated as sacred beings, ancestors reborn from heaven, until they lose their milk teeth. After that they are expected to learn to live like adults. They receive a formal school education, but learn Balinese ways by joining freely in adult activities. There are several childhood ceremonies. On the 42nd day after a baby's birth mother and child are ritually purified by a priest. The baby is festooned with anklets, bracelets and necklaces as amulets to protect him from evil spirits, and promote his proper development. He is usually named at a ceremony three months later. On his first birthday, which is 210 days from birth in the Balinese ritual calendar, his parents hold a big ceremony, with a feast for guests. Elaborate offerings are made in the family temple. The child, dressed in brocade and gold jewelry has his head shaved by a priest, leaving only a tuft of hair on his forehead. The feet of this 'small inhabitant of heaven' are ritually placed on the ground for the first time, for up till now he has always been carried everywhere. Children are weaned on their third birthday.

At adolescence children's teeth should be filed ceremonially: only evil spirits or animals have pointed or fang-like teeth. But often it is too expensive. Fees have to be paid for the specialist as well as for the customary offerings and entertainments, and it may well be delayed until marriage, or simply avoided. For girls there is a further puberty ceremony. They are considered unclean at the time of their first period, and must be secluded until the time has passed. Each girl is then purified by a priest, and her coming to womanhood is celebrated with a feast, music and dancing at her home.

Life's most important ceremonies are funeral rituals, performed by kinsmen. When a person dies his soul is thought to leave his body, but still to be anchored to earthly things. His body is buried in the cemetery, the realm of the underworld, until his relations are able to proceed with the necessary rituals to send the soul from earth to paradise. The life cycle can then begin again with rebirth. But at the same time death pollutes the community, and weakens it, and cleansing rituals are needed. Poor people have simpler ceremonies.

As for all important activities, an auspicious day is selected from the ritual calendar by the priest. The dead man's remains are dug up, and his soul is induced to enter a palm leaf effigy of himself. This effigy is carried in a

During a *kris* dance an evil *rangda* puts a spell on the dancers who enter a trance and stab themselves. They are miraculously unharmed.

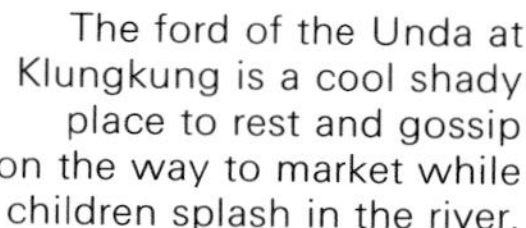

A solitary scarecrow stands guard in a field. There is little to spare for birds as population grows and food imports increase.

The ford of the Unda at Klungkung is a cool shady place to rest and gossip on the way to market while children splash in the river.

Ketut Renend is the oldest and best dance teacher in Denpasar where from childhood girls are trained in the sinuous art of the dance.

A procession of women in the village of Mas carry 'high offerings' to a presentation ceremony in the temple courtyard.

festive procession to the high priest for blessing the evening before the cremation. A party follows at his kinsmen's home with food, music, dancing and shadow plays. The next morning everyone assembles gaily, and the effigy and the remains are placed in a tall bamboo-framed tower, and carried in a procession to the cremation ground, being twisted and turned to confuse evil spirits. The remains are put into a special coffin carved like a bull, cow or lion, depending on the dead person's caste and sex, and everything is burnt and then cast into the sea with a final ceremony. The entire set of ceremonies is repeated 42 days later with an effigy in place of the corpse, and then the family can be sure that the soul of the deceased lies in paradise.

Village life contributes to the general sense of social order. Villages are usually built on mountain spurs, and laid out in a regular pattern. The main street runs down the slope, with houses on either side. At the top of the village is the temple where the founding ancestors are worshipped, and at the lower end are the cemetery and temples for the dead. At the central crossroads is the village temple where rituals to protect the village are performed, and there is also an assembly hall, a shed for cockfighting and an ornate tower, housing the wooden slit gongs to call people to their duties. A sacred banyan tree gives shade for talking, trading and playing music.

Most villages or hamlets are extremely independent, although within the national administrative system, and are sometimes described as village republics. All married adults are expected to take a responsible part in village life, and there are strictly enforced penalties for non-conformity to village laws and customs. An assembly of married men, under a committee of five elders (who have a five year term of office) decides all village affairs, from worship and property disputes to festivals.

Farming is the mainstay of the village economy, depending on water buffalo and ox-plows. In central Bali wet rice is cultivated in a complex system of irrigated terraced fields – one of the wonders of Bali. There the climate is so favorable and the volcanic soil so rich that the yearly crops of wet rice are produced. Maize and vegetables are the main crops on non-irrigated land and there are also coffee plots and coconut groves, with cattle, pigs, chickens and ducks. Farming is run by agricultural co-operatives whose members are all the farmers whose fields are served by one irrigation system.

Meetings of the co-operative – which enforces a conformity on its members – are compulsory. An elected committee organizes work and ritual offerings to the rice goddess Dewi Sri. It arranges the great harvest festivals, when each family makes its own straw Rice Mother to carry in the procession to the granaries, to

A ferocious *rangda*, or witch performs in the Legong dance, the most famous of all Bali's many beautiful dances.

Graceful girls follow the *rangda*. To the Balinese religion, history, folklore, mythology and art are all expressed in their dances.

Girls fall in a trance after whirling round for 20 minutes. Here performed for tourists, this dance originated to benefit a sick person.

An old priest leads his successor in a procession to the temple in Denpasar for the three-day-long inauguration ceremony.

(Center) The new priest and his wife are carried home in state at the end of three days after being ceremonialy washed and robed.

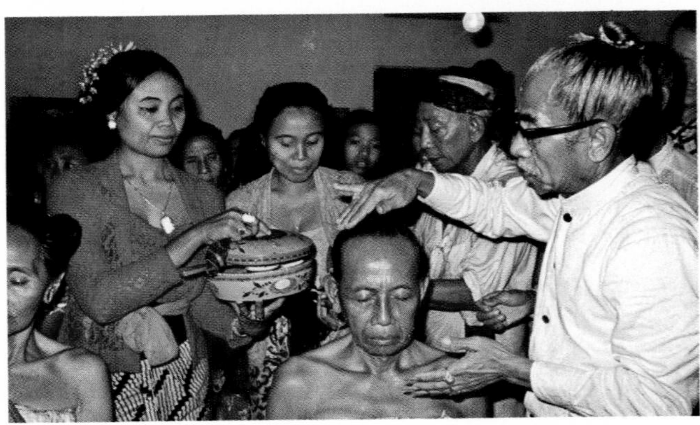

After washing, the priest has his head oiled and his hair arranged for the first time into a top-knot denoting his new status.

protect the spirit of the rice.

Bali is famous for many other festivals too. In the village temple the key event of the year is the celebration of its *odalan* day, the day when the spirit of its patron deity first entered it. Temples are resting places for the spirits of the gods when they visit the earth, and consist of two compounds decorated with statues. There are no idols. In the upper courtyard there are various shrines for prayer to the mountains, ancestors and the 'interpreters' of the deities, and various gods. There is a seat to receive the sun god, Surya. In the lower courtyard ceremonial food is cooked, and there is a rest house for worshippers and a bandstand for the *gamelan* orchestra.

Preparations for the *odalan* day begin long beforehand. The temple is decorated with flowers and hanging umbrellas and streamers. Then on the day, everyone dresses up and the women bring carefully arranged offerings to the temple where the men are preparing festive food. In the afternoon there are prayers for the whole community and the temple's guardian priest makes offerings to the gods. The spirits of the gods are persuaded to enter sacred images which are then picked up and carried in cheerful procession to the sea or to the nearest large river. They are ritually bathed and then brought back to the village. Rituals continue throughout the night. Mediums enter trances to communicate with the deities and divine their satisfaction with the offerings. At the same time there are feasts and dancing, music and plays. At dawn the following day, a ceremony for the adoration of the rising sun marks the end of the festival.

The Nyepi festival takes place at the spring equinox. For the Balinese it is the time to clear out the devils from the community so that the new year may begin clean and fresh. The last morning of the old year is traditionally spent watching Bali's national sport – cockfighting – which generates great excitement and heavy gambling. Then, in the afternoon, the villagers bring offerings to the village crossroads where altars and seats have already been erected. Some of the offerings are for the great gods, some for the ancestors, and some for the evil spirits. The priests dedicate the offerings to the various spirits, and then turn on the demons who have been lured by the great offerings and drive them from the village with powerful magical incantations. Later, after prayers, household heads are given new fire, holy water and consecrated rice for the new year. The rest of the night is spent – especially by the children – making as much noise as possible around the village to drive away the devils. The next day is the day of Nyepi itself. It is a day of stillness, when no work is permitted, and no fires or lights allowed. Today in the towns people actually go visiting, but the food is still prepared in advance. On the following day fire and light are permitted. Work, however, does not begin until this day has passed.

The most important holidays of the Balinese year are those in the two weeks or so around the days of *Galungan* and *Kuningan* when the spirits of the ancestors return to the homes of their living relatives for ten days. It is a time for rich offerings in the household and clan temples, and at the temples of the dead in the village. It is also a time for dressing up in new clothes, for visits, feasts, music, plays and dancing. The processions are gay, full of color, and enlivened by the cavorting of carnival monsters.

Although these great religious festivals display and help maintain the many arts of the Balinese, all Balinese art is not religious. Craftsmanship is admired for its own sake – as both a hobby and a profession. Everyone on Bali appears to have some artistic skill, and every village seems to excel in one particular field. A wide variety of simple but beautiful everyday implements and utensils were traditionally made by hand, mostly in bamboo. At the same time, intricate wood and stone carvings were made to decorate homes, temples, palaces and public buildings. Artists produced detailed, beautiful and formal paintings of episodes in such stories as the great epics of the Ramayana and the Mahabaratta. Then, in the 1920s, the island was 'discovered' by European artists, led by a Belgian painter named Adrien Le Majeur who settled in Bali and married a Balinese girl. The Balinese learnt something both from these artists and from the tourists who followed. New art styles began to emerge to cater for the tourist trade. Wooden statuettes of great elegance and skill found a ready market, and Balinese painting became more realistic and less formal, portraying scenes from everyday life. Even newer styles of painting and wood-carving are especially vigorous today, while other arts and crafts have remained more traditional. Iron, brass, bronze, gold and silver are all used, for example, to produce attractive jewelry, richly ornamented *krises* (sacred daggers with wavy blades) and most of the instruments of the *gamelan* orchestras. In a few communities Balinese women still produce some of the most intricate weaving in south-east Asia; among the best specimens are the warp and weft tie-dye *gringsing* of Tenganan, and the gold and silver threaded brocades of Klungkung. It is the women too who have made an art of the temple offerings of food and flowers, and of making the pretty *cili* figures and *lamak* banners from palm leaf strips used at all festivals.

Every ceremony, whether the simple childhood rites, marriage celebrations, great mortuary rituals, rice festivals, temple birthdays or calendar feasts, includes music, dancing and drama as a regular part of the event. In the *wayang lemah,* a short puppet play performed during the daytime, the drama is actually a prescribed ritual to drive out evil spirits. The recited text tells the Chalonarang story of how the evil widow Rangda and her witches, in alliance with Durga the goddess of death, caused many troubles before they were defeated and destroyed by a holy man. The popular *wayang kulit,* or shadow theater also has something of this ritual aspect, and the puppeteer, the *dalang,* always makes offerings

A bull-shaped coffin, showing the caste of the dead person, is borne in a joyful procession to the cremation ground by the whole village.

before the performance and recites magic verses as he takes the puppets from their box. The *dalang* is a scholar well versed in the classics and his stories are heroic tales from the Balinese versions of the great Hindu epics. The puppets are made from thin hide intricately cut and carefully painted and gilded. Their silhouettes are cast on a screen by a lamp. The performance often lasts all night.

Music is provided by the *gamelan* orchestras. Every village tries to support a number of *gamelan* to play at its feasts and ceremonies. Each *gamelan* will have its own club, and each will specialize in a particular repertoire, The orchestra may have a large number of instruments – drums, gongs, bells, cymbals, xylophones, metallophones, flutes, violins – each a work of great beauty and often decorated with fine carvings and gold leaf. The full orchestra for a concert has between 20 and 40 players, but other occasions will demand a different number of musicians and a different combination of instruments. The music, based on a five-tone scale, is much brighter than Javanese *gamelan,* and more pleasing to a western ear unaccustomed to so much percussion.

Live drama is also popular and village clubs specialize in a number of different kinds of plays. The *wayang wong* plays are based on the same stories as the *wayang kulit,* mighty epics in which noble princes clash with demon kings in the perpetual battle between good and evil. They are accompanied by the same *wayang* music, and the parts are played by live actors using masks. For its sophisticated élite, the Balinese hold operettas and historical plays spoken in the Kawi language.

In Bali, the most popular dramas are dance dramas, and the Balinese excel in dancing. In this, their natural beauty, graceful carriage and flair for dress find full expression. Particularly splendid are the dances based on the Chalonarang story. In the usual dance version the forces of good are assisted by the *barong* (an enormous Chinese lion mask worn by two men like a pantomine horse). The Rangda, a hideous and evil old witch with matted hair and pendulous breasts, plays all kinds of cunning tricks to defeat the forces of good. In the end the matter is left unresolved, even though the witch's *kris* dancers in a trance turn their *kris* knives upon themselves in a final frenzied orgy of stabbing. They are unharmed even though they plunge the *kris* deep into their flesh in a dramatic demonstration of religious scorn for mere human life and human senses. The *barong* also turns up on other occasions, especially at Galungan time, and there are other *kris* dances, some performed in a trance state as part of temple rituals. Another favorite dance is the *kecak*. A few actors perform the scenes from the

If the time is inauspicious for cremation, the corpse is buried and the soul must wait until the right time to be ritually released in cremation.

As the burial is 'stolen' and the soul not released, the corpse must be allowed to 'breathe' through this bamboo tube until cremation.

Ramayana where the hero is under attack by demons, and monkeys come to his rescue. The actors are entirely surrounded by a large male chorus who chant throughout *kecak, kecak,* over and over. Eventually the chorus becomes the opposed armies of monkeys and demons for the great battle. In dim lamplight, the hypnotic chant, the massed swaying bodies advancing and retreating, the simple sarongs of black and white checks, the flowers behind ears make this a compelling spectacle.

The graceful *legong* dance is in complete contrast. This classical ballet is performed by two young girls in rich and elegant costumes. Their stylized dance tells a story of the abduction of a princess by a prince and of her rescue by her betrothed. But the story itself is subordinate to the elegance of the dance and the beauty of the music. Here fingers, hands, arms, shoulders and eyes all must significantly be combined with foot, body and head in the standard attitudes necessary for the dance.

Other dances associated with the temple festivals are the *rejang,* a processional dance for the unmarried girls of the village, *gabor* and *mendet* women's dances during which offerings are made, and *baris* drill dances for older men, of which the most famous was the warrior dance. In secular dances, fashions come and go, but the *joged* and *kebyar* have been particularly popular. In *joged* a single girl dances in classic style while boys come in turn to accompany her. *Kebyar* is a graceful solo dance performed in the seated position by a young man.

Most of Bali's actors, dancers and musicians are not professional. Any fees they might earn are plowed back into their village clubs to buy the costly *gamelan* instruments and dance costumes. Nevertheless standards are high, probably because many Balinese are willing to dedicate themselves to training despite other onerous responsibilities. Most Balinese lead very active lives, but the rewards are obvious. Religion and community form a totality which allows for a full life for even the poorest among them. In this lies the beauty of Bali and its powerful attraction for the urban and industrialized world.

The right time for cremation, when at last it arrives, is a time of rejoicing. The dead man's personal things are burnt with him.

Kayan
Borneo

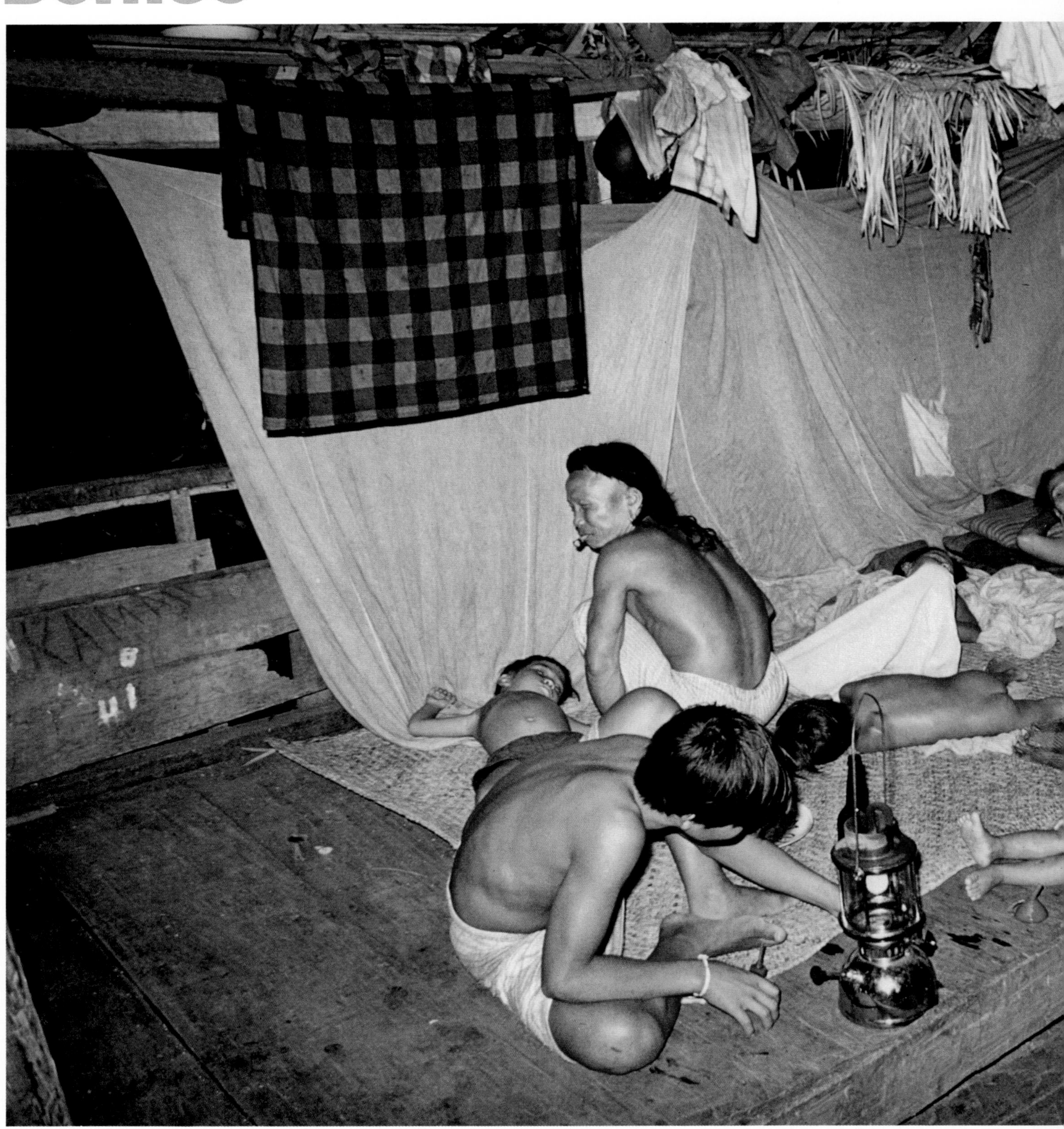

Once a year after the headhunting ceremonies, people sleep for one night on the veranda in front of the long house.

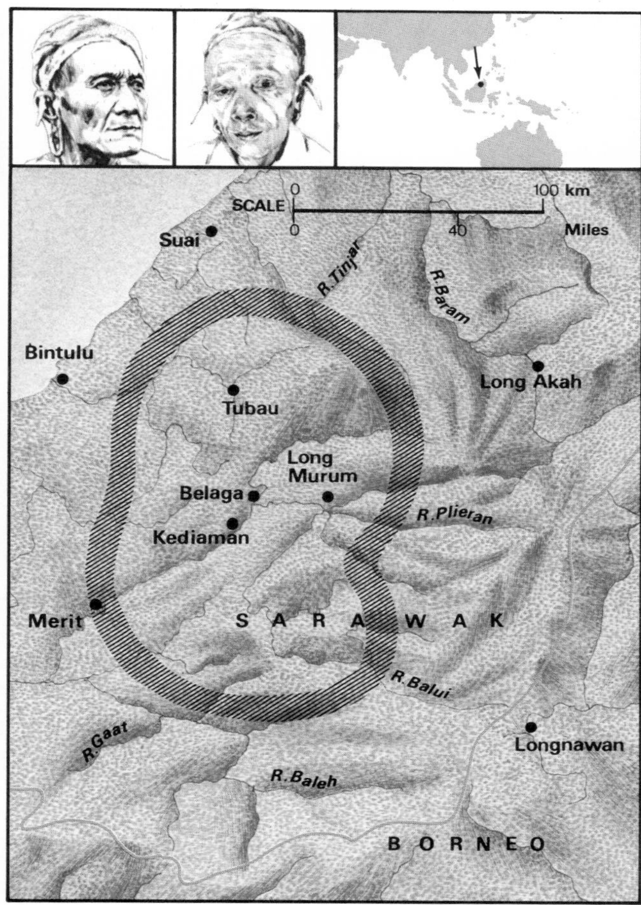

In the tropical jungle which covers central Borneo live several groups of people, some of whom are nomadic and others in permanent villages. Along the river banks, scattered throughout the area are the communities of one of the settled groups, the Kayan. Until they scattered in several river basins over two hundred years ago the Kayan lived clustered together in one area of Kalimantan (the Indonesian side of Borneo).

Although the various segments of the Kayan are widely separated they still share a way of life that is largely the same. Each Kayan village consists of just one house, a long house, an imposing structure built of iron wood five to fifteen feet from the ground and as much as 200 to 400 feet in length. In separate apartments in each of these edifices live ten to thirty families each of about ten people: grandparents, one or two of their married children and their grandchildren. Not until the children of brothers and sisters living together approach marriageable age do they divide their common possessions and set up separate households. Each apartment has two small sparsely furnished rooms: a main room, covered by rattan mats with a raised platform on one

Each year, before the rice is sown, a pig must be sacrificed by a Kayan priest in front of the chief's room at the farm.

side where the unmarried men sleep and where women sit when the harvest is over weaving rattan mats and baskets. The room is made even smaller by the addition of sleeping partitions for parents and unmarried daughters. There is a kitchen with little else than a fireplace, bamboo water containers and a clay hearth with three stones inside for the cooking pots to rest on. Above the hearth is a rack where firewood is stored. Often strips of pork hang from the rack curing in the smoke. On the walls fishing, hunting and farming equipment hang on bone or wooden hooks. Family rooms are dark and smoky and anything but quiet. Babies, hens and dogs swarm over the floor while old women sit gossiping, stopping only to kick a hungry dog away from the food cooking on the hearth. A gallery runs the length of the long house outside the apartment. It is the main thoroughfare and the place where all the public life of the village goes on. There are wide platforms on the outer edge where men sit gossiping and smoking. Outside each apartment are large wooden mortars where young girls pound rice for the daily meals. On the walls of the gallery are hung wooden boxes where the men keep their war cloaks and shields, safe from insects, dogs and children.

In these impressive structures the Kayan live for only half the year. They spend the rest of the year on their

A few days after a patch of jungle has been cleared and burnt, the men make holes in the earth in which the women sow the seed.

About two months are spent weeding. It is hard work and some of the women use a screen to protect their backs from the sun.

farms, where they cultivate rice as their principal crop, and live in relative privacy in farmhouses that may accommodate one or several families. They grow the rice, not in rice swamps, but on the hills by shifting cultivation, each year clearing and tilling a new patch of land in the jungle. Before cultivating an area a second time, they leave the land fallow for 10 to 30 years until it has been covered once more with trees, so as not to exhaust the land. There is no permanent ownership of land: the produce of a field belongs to a single household, but it may in the future be used by any other members of the village. This is only possible because each community has a large territory. Farm work is done by co-operative groups.

Each year the Kayan fell a new patch of jungle, leave it to dry for a month, and then set it on fire so as to simultaneously clear the field and produce fertilizer. The rice fields stand on steep slopes, as there is no flat land. The men dibble holes in the ground in which the women throw rice seeds. Although felling and burning the trees is strictly men's work, men and women otherwise work equally hard at sowing, weeding and harvesting.

As well as rice the Kayan grow tapioca, mainly as pig-feed, and a strong tobacco which they smoke heavily, rolled in wild banana leaves. The adults chew a mildly narcotic plug of areca nut, lime and betel leaf. They eat coconuts and bananas, slaughter and eat their pigs and chickens only at feasts and ceremonies and otherwise eat game and fish. Wild boar, which they track with their dogs, is their principal source of red meat, but their main source of protein is fish, usually dried.

The men are out fishing, with cast-nets or floating nets, while the women are busy at home preparing food, usually a bland dish, simply cooked. The women spend much time pounding and sifting the rice, feeding the pigs and chickens, cutting and drying the tobacco.

From the virgin jungle which covers most of the area, they collect rattan, various resins, aromatic woods, bezoar stones (a concretion found in the gall-bladder of certain animals credited with medicinal powers), heads of hornbill birds (the horn is regarded as an aphrodisiac) and other jungle produce. Usually the Kayan prefer to leave to their nomadic neighbors the gathering of these products which they exchange for cloth and iron at a handsome profit. In turn the Kayan then sell them to the Chinese traders and buy cloth, iron, salt and other luxuries with the proceeds. Although the Kayan live far inland, they have been trading for decades and have accumulated many valuable objects: bronze gongs and cannons, large jars and glass beads, which may be used for bride-price payments.

Skilled Kayan smiths used to smelt their own iron; now more often they buy iron bars to make adzes, machetes and knives.

The women catch fish stunned by vegetable poison, a method which is used only a few times a year.

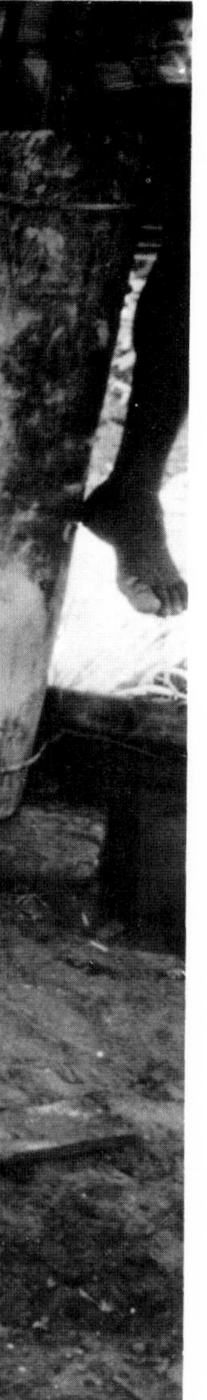

When girls are ten years old, and when boys are a little older, they start to help their parents. Girls marry between the ages of 13 and 18. Boys marry a few years older. It is forbidden to marry a second cousin or any closer relative, but most Kayan marry spouses from the same village. Although the Kayan do not forbid polygamy, it is exceptional. Provided her parents do not oppose her choice a girl can marry whoever she chooses: parents do not arrange marriages. After the marriage ceremony to which every member of the long house comes, the bridegroom goes to live with his wife's family of which he becomes a full member. He may not set up a separate room. Couples who have no daughters find themselves alone as their sons marry and are left with nobody to help them in their old age. In this case after their son has been married for several years they will often ask his wife's parents if he may come back with her and settle permanently with them. They give the girl's parents a bride-price if they agree. It is paid nowadays partly in cash and partly in valuable objects, and ranges in total value between $75 and $175 – a large sum for people who practise a subsistence economy.

Men take all the community decisions and have a higher status than women. The Kayan also have great respect for age: the word of the elder members of the community carries most weight.

Kayan society is organized throughout in four ranks, each with different duties and privileges. Although it is preferable to marry a person of one's own rank, it is permitted to do otherwise. The highest of the four ranks, from which the chief is chosen, are the *maren*, the 'high aristocrats'. Each long house has usually one, sometimes two, *maren* families, from which the chief is chosen. A chief is succeeded by his most able son or, if he has no sons, by his son-in-law. A son who expects to succeed his father as chief marries a wife of his own rank from another village, and after living in her village for a few years brings her back to his own long house. The bride-price, which is extremely high—sometimes as much as $1,000 – is paid half by his family and half by the members of his long house.

The ruling family is set apart from the other members of the community. Commoners work the chief's farms, build his implements and boats, and occasionally supply him with meat. The chiefs do a little work, such as hunting, which they consider enjoyable. Their womenfolk do some domestic tasks, but rarely go to their farms. They have a great deal of leisure, which they spend in fine handicrafts or trading with the nomads.

The chiefs own slaves. There are two degrees of slavery. Some of them belong directly to the chief's household and the entire product of their work goes to him. The others are economically independent and owe only part of their time to the chief. In the past the Kayan made slaves of captives taken in war. Their number is now rapidly dwindling, as the practice has been banned by the government.

In between the *maren* and the commoners are the *hipuy*, the 'low aristocrats', who are associated with the ruling class for ceremonial purposes; although usually wealthier than the majority of the population they work and live as commoners.

The commoners form the bulk of the population. They are free men who nevertheless have to give some of their time in unpaid labor to the chief. A commoner family cannot leave a long house to settle into another without paying a large fine to the chief. If a commoner accumulates wealth and involves himself in community matters he can gain status and in this way can achieve prominence in his long house. The powerful commoners can apply pressure to restrain the chief if he makes unreasonable demands. They can also solve small conflicts.

Community matters and important offences are beyond their range and are discussed in public meetings in which the older men are the most active participants. The chief will normally accept most of the elders' suggestions, but he is not bound to do so. Above the level of the community the Kayan have no formal political organization although long houses are linked in many ways. Chiefs are related by marriage, and visit each other to discuss regional matters.

Before the Kayan came under the power of an outside administration the chiefs of a few large long houses managed to establish their influence beyond their own community to ally themselves against common enemies, and several long houses followed their leadership. The Kayan managed to expand rapidly into areas of Sarawak which they coveted and displace the earlier occupants there. After they settled there they continued to have skirmishes with each other and with other groups often as a result of their practice of headhunting. Although the Kayan captured the heads of their enemies principally because they believed that in doing so they would bring spiritual well-being to their community, they also found that taking head-trophies when they fought to expand their territory had the further advantage of frightening their enemies and inducing them to submit. After they

Communities live beside a river in a long house built on stilts up to 15 feet high, surrounded by barns and storehouses.

Headhunting trophies like this skullcap still feature in Kayan religion, though the practice ceased early in the 20th century.

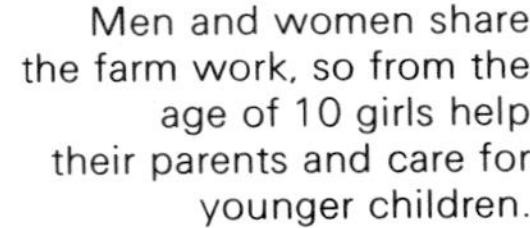

Men and women share the farm work, so from the age of 10 girls help their parents and care for younger children.

had achieved their object the Kayan headhunted only for religious reasons, and as little as possible. And, to reduce the chance of reprisals, they took heads stealthily, from remote groups. By the end of the 19th century, headhunting was rare. It had virtually disappeared in 1924 when several peace-making gatherings were organized both in Sarawak and in the then Dutch area of Borneo.

The Kayan devote much of their time, thoughts and talk to religion. A male god, Lake' Tenangan, his wife, Doh Tenangan, and her sister Dipuy head their divine hierarchy. They live in a series of longhouses together with a number of spirits in another world. It is through the wrath of such a spirit that a person falls ill, for the angry spirit snatches one of his souls away. It is the duty of the Kayan priest to fetch it back. These spirits can also help human beings. Material success and authority are taken as manifestations of spiritual help. Kayan rituals and ceremonies are centered upon rice cultivation and the curing of illnesses. There are other kinds of spirits in this world, some of them indifferent to humans, others dangerous. Supernatural beings are also thought to live in large isolated boulders which the Kayan approach with dread. The most powerful of the spirits of this world, and the most frightening is the Thunder, although the Kayan he visits in dreams may thereafter be certain of a successful life.

The old religion was extremely exacting. A large number of animals were taboo: for example, deer, wild ox, turtle, monitor lizard, and several species of birds and fish – should be regarded as taboo. There were also special prohibitions for farming, hunting, building a a new house, headhunting and every variety of activity. These endless restrictions greatly limited the Kayan in their daily pursuits. It was believed that if a person laughed at animals it would so arouse the anger of the Thunder who would turn him to stone.

During the 1940s, a man from a neighboring group, the Kenyah, claimed to be inspired in a dream by the Head-Goddess, and he initiated a religious reform which the Kenyah and Kayan rapidly accepted. He announced that the Head-Goddess was taking away from her sister earthly matters which had been her realm until then, and that she had decided that ceremonies would be simplified, and that all food taboos and auguries would disappear. After converting his own people, the prophet brought the new faith to the Kayan.

Nevertheless Kayan rituals like their basic beliefs

Possessed by his spirit helpers and with his head covered in a cloth, a shaman draws sickness from his patient by pinching it out of the stomach.

follow the traditional pattern. There are two kinds of religious specialists – the priests who perform the curing ceremonies and the complex ceremonies related to each phase of rice cultivation and the shamans.

The Kayan perform communal ceremonies in the afternoon on the gallery, in front of the room of the chief. They last for an hour or so. A specified number of eggs are placed in a brass tray; occasionally pigs and chickens are sacrificed.

These ceremonies are held at the start of the ritual sowing and harvesting, and in thanksgiving at the end of the harvest. Other rituals are to purify the members of the community from spiritual dangers, when a person has died, for example, or if there is an epidemic. Every year men still participate in the headhunting ceremony, affecting to 'kill' a head-trophy kept specially for this purpose.

Several times a year a family will ask a priest to perform rituals for them, either to cure a sick member of the family or simply for their general wellbeing. They hold these rituals at night, as this is when the spirits are awake. After a few prayers inside their room, they go to the gallery, and there they lay offerings of cloth on a cross-shaped altar, in front of which they place eggs. After the ceremony, the pieces of cloth and the eggs will be stored for future religious use. The priest addresses a chicken or a pig, who will take the prayers of the humans to the spirits and the divine couple. The animal is sacrificed, cooked and eaten, and the ceremony resumes with the priest singing for several hours, describing the journey of his soul to the other world as it searches for the patient's wandering soul.

Naming ceremonies, marriages and funerals are also part of the duties of priests, who have a higher status than shamans, because their activity is an art form as well as a religious practice: they sing religious texts in a poetical language, and people flock to listen to those gifted with a good voice. The shamans perform only one kind of curing ritual, which does not involve the journey of their soul to the other world. The shaman goes into a trance, and his body is inhabited by his spirit-helpers, who direct him to the source of the illness, which he sucks or pinches out of the patient's body. Priest and shamans receive fees for their services, without which they would be in spiritual danger. Men and women can equally assume religious duties, and they receive their calling in dreams from spirits.

The Kayan occasionally gather at night on the gallery to sing non-religious epics and other songs. The other art forms are best expressed during the harvest festival, which lasts several days. People bedecked with head-dresses, bead, hornbill feathers, and other fineries dance to music played on a *sape*, a three stringed instrument. It is the occasion for lavish consumption of their potent rice-wine. As soon as the harvest festival is finished, they go back to work to start a new year, and new farms.

Glossary peoples of Indonesia, Philippines and Malaysia

The Malay world is formed by the Malay peninsula and a great crescent of islands curving round from Sumatra through Java and the Celebes up to the Philippines enclosing Borneo, Singapore and dotting out in islands across to New Guinea. This world is divided into four political units – Malaysia which includes Malaya, Sarawak and Sabah; Singapore (which broke away from Malaysia in 1965); Indonesia which includes Java, Sumatra, Borneo, Bali, Celebes and West Irian in New Guinea; and the Philippines, an archipelago of 7,100 islands, the largest of which are Luzon and Mindanao. The people who inhabit this world are mostly Malays or descendants of Malays; Chinese, concentrated particularly in Malaya and Singapore; Indians in Malaya; and a few small groups of other peoples such as the proto-Malays and Negritos.

The first people to reach Malaya were migrant peoples of the prehistoric period from the Asian land mass. The negrito descendants of these aborigine migrants still live isolated in the central jungles of Malaya and in the extreme south of Thailand. Some can also be found in the mountainous parts of eastern and western Luzon and in the north-east of Mindanao. They are an unsophisticated people who gather their food from the forests and hunt with blow pipes and poisoned darts.

Proto-Malays are so called because they arrived before Malays and share many common elements with them, although in general they have longer heads, broader noses and are stockier in build. Some true descendants of the proto-Malays remain, like the Jakun who live in small scattered groups deep in the southern and eastern jungles of Malaya, and the Ifugao of Luzon in the Philippines. Most of the proto-Malays were absorbed into the next wave of southern mongoloid migrants from the north, to produce the modern Malays. They settled in the Malay peninsula and spread out into Indonesia and the Philippines where over the centuries they have mixed with other peoples and cultures. A majority of the Malayan Malays are peasant farmers who live in the north and east where they grow rice to feed themselves, or are fishermen. In southern and central Malaya, the Malay smallholder is frequently the owner of land under rubber or coconut cultivation. Once Malays were disinclined to work as wage labor but today increasing numbers leave their villages *(kampongs)* and seek jobs as transport drivers, policemen or as civil servants. Before colonization by the British in the last century, Malays had a reputation as warriors and pirates – and for a tendency to run *amok*. Other characteristics have since prevailed: by and large Malays today are quiet, gentle and courteous and play a relatively small role in urban life, where the Chinese call the tune.

Filipinos are now a distinctive race with an admixture of Chinese, Spanish, and American blood. Most are farmers who grow rice, maize and sweet potatoes for food on smallholdings, while commercial crops intended for export like tobacco, coffee, sugar cane, coconuts and manila hemp are cultivated on larger estates. There are minerals – but they are not mined extensively. Since World War II industry has expanded and Filipinos now work in factories producing textiles, chemicals, steel, aluminium and rubber goods. Filipinos have been greatly influenced by the USA which controlled the Philippines from 1898 to 1964.

Modern Indonesians are a mixture of Malay, Melanesian and Papuan and are not a homogenous race. There are over 300 ethnic groups who speak over 250 distinct languages all belonging to the Malayo-Polynesian family. But most modern Indonesians are recognizable by their short stature, light to dark brown skin, sleek black hair, wide noses and thick lips.

The Chinese have throughout their history been in close contact with countries to the south of China. They came to Malaya, Indonesia and the Philippines to trade spices and other goods. The majority of the Chinese are descendants of immigrants who arrived from south-eastern China from 1830 to 1930. They are predominantly townsmen and have almost complete control of local wholesale and retail trades, a large section of the tin mining industry, banking and the rubber industry. In Malaya large numbers of Chinese came between 1870 and 1930 to work the rubber plantations and tin mines. Their descendants continue in this same role, although many have become farmers and traders. Before Singapore opted out of Malayasia, the Chinese formed nearly half the population: today, some 38 per cent of Malayans are Chinese.

Indonesia also imported some Chinese labor, but on a smaller scale: they form some two per cent. Yet Indonesians have resented the Chinese dominance of trade, commerce and industry and the government has tried to curb their activities. In 1959 President Sukarno expelled the Chinese from the rural areas and indeed many were killed during the massacres after the abortive *coup d'état* by left-wing and communist forces in 1965. It is in Singapore that the Chinese dominate and nearly three quarters of the population are of Chinese descent. And it is they who are responsible for turning Singapore into the prosperous, busy manufacturing center and port that it is today.

Indian immigration to Malaya began as a source of labor for Malaya's expanding economy, particularly with the development of the rubber industry from 1900 onwards. The immigrants came from the Tamil, Telugu and Malayalam-speaking areas of south India, but also from Punjab and Bengal. Their descendants still work on the rubber plantations, but an increasing number take jobs in the tin mines and on the wharfs and railways. Indians work as doctors, lawyers and in white collar jobs. In north Borneo there are only about 2,000 Indians who work as general and textile merchants in the cities and some in the oil fields.

ALAS-GAYO *Population:* 85,000. Language group: Sumatran. There are about 70,000 Gayo and 15,000 Alas who live in isolated inland groups in mountainous north Sumatra. Apart from their staples (wet rice and maize) they grow vegetables, cotton, sugar cane and tobacco. They eat dried fish and deer meat, and raise some cattle. They build higgledy-piggledy arrangements of long communal dwellings on piles along the rivers. Inside the houses are divided into family apartments, a men's gallery and a women's gallery. Although they are almost totally surrounded by the Atjehnese (q.v.) they know little of Islam.

ALOR-SOLAR ISLANDERS *Population:* 200,000. Language group: Bima-Sumba. The islands stretch 150 miles east from Flores to Timor. The five largest are Solar (population 40,000), Adonara (30,000), Lomblem (40,000), Pantar (10,000), and Alor (60,000). The natives of these rocky islands live in small villages (usually built on defensive mountain sites) of several communal houses each occupied by a group of relations. They raise pigs and chickens, but water buffalo and horses are mostly owned by rajas. On Lomblem many are fishermen and many grow copra for export, as well as dry rice, maize and beans, their staple crops. On ceremonial occasions like weddings, burials and house-building they dance and exchange the local currency of pigs, gongs and *mokos* (highly-prized metal kettle drums). The traditional religions survive to a degree although there are Muslim communities along the coast.

AMBONESE *Population:* 100,000. Language groups: Moluccan Malay, Dutch. The small Ambon Islands lie just south of western Ceram. They were originally inhabited by a small dispersed population of shifting cultivators divided into independent tribes. These people have had a great deal of contact with the west, and their language has been replaced by Malay and Dutch. The islanders live mostly in small villages. Each important family has its own title of honor and owns a sacred stream, a sacred stone and several plots of land where they cultivate sago and pepper. They also grow rice, maize and coffee using the plots until they are exhausted. But their staple, sago, comes mainly from Ceram. Copra and cloves are produced for export. Since the island became the Dutch administrative center of the Moluccas many Ambonese have been educated to a high level and live and work throughout Indonesia in schools, hospitals and the civil service.

APAYO-ISNEG *Population:* 13,000. Language group: Isneg. Several related groups of Apayo-Isneg live scattered over the far north-west of the Philippine island of Luzon. They grow rice (their staple), corn and tropical roots on shifting plots of land. They hunt, fish, rear cattle and trade tobacco and other produce in the lowlands. They live either in scattered dwellings or in small hamlets.

ARABS *Population:* 100,000. Language group: Arabic. Although Muslim Arab traders and merchants have visited the area from Nias (q.v.) to the Philippines, for many hundreds of years, few have settled permanently. Most of the Arabs who now live in these islands are from the Hadramaut region of central south Arabia. Nearly 60 per cent live in Java-Madura (q.v.), the rest are scattered throughout the islands. They work mainly as retail traders or commercial middlemen, and are well integrated with the native peoples.

ARU ISLANDERS *Population:* 40,000. Language group: Ambon-Timor. This southernmost group of the Moluccas is in the Arafura sea to the south of New Guinea. The native islanders (the Pata-lima and the Pata-siwa) are of mixed Papuan and Malay stock. Their land is communally owned but mostly uncultivated: the islanders hunt and explore it for wild sago (their staple food) and other forest produce. They also hunt birds of Paradise for their magnificent plumes. Their closely crowded houses are entered by a trap door in the center of the floor. In the center of the village there is usually a shed, the home of a spirit that protects the community, to whom offerings are made. Most retain their indigenous beliefs although a few are Christian or Muslim.

ATJEHNESE *Population:* 2 million. Language group: Sumatran. The Atjehnese live in the coastland of northern Sumatra. Once a series of independent tribes the Atjehnese were welded into quasi-national unity during their war with the Dutch in 1873. The present population is mixed with people from Malacca, Batakland, Nias (q.v.), who came as slaves, Javanese, Hindus and Arabs. As well as staples (wet and dry rice) they cultivate sugar cane, pepper and fruit trees. Meat is only eaten on festive occasions. Many are skilled craftsmen and extremely able traders. The Atjehnese have shamans but they also strictly observe the laws of Islamic religion and custom, and many go on annual pilgrimages to Mecca. In the early 17th century there was a 'Golden Era' in this kingdom under the Sultan Iskandar Muda who had a trade monopoly with the Dutch.

ATONI *Population:* 600,000. Language group: Ambon-Timor. The Atoni live in the mountainous areas of central and western Timor, an island at the eastern end of the Lesser Sunda Islands. They call themselves Atoni Pah Meto (people of the dry land) and avoid the sea and coast. The hamlets and fields of these people who practise shifting cultivation lie along ridges and slopes near sources of water. The Atoni supplement their rice diet with sorghum. They breed cattle, horses and water buffalo (a mark of social standing). They prize self-reliance: 'one man, one field' is the general rule. The only craft at which they excel is weaving. Since the 15th century the Atoni have traded sandalwood.

BADJAWANESE see SIKA

BADUI *Population:* 2,000. Language group: Javanese. The Badui are a semi-isolated people who live in west Java (q.v.). They are thought to be descendants of an earlier people in Java. Little is known about them but their religion, a form of degenerate Hinduism, stresses ancestor worship and forbids them to wear ornaments and use foreign (non-Badui) articles.

BAGABO *Population:* 21,000. Language group: Bagabo. The Bagabo live on the steep slopes of the volcanic Mount Apo and on the shores of the Davao Gulf on Mindanao Island, Philippines. Most are farmers who grow dry land rice and enough Manila hemp to trade on the coast. They live in one-roomed houses with bamboo walls, raised off the ground. Six large gongs hang near the center of the local ruler's house and are played at all festivities. They have been influenced by Mohammedanism, but until quite recently they made yearly human sacrifices to the spirits Mandarangan and Darago, the patrons of warriors, who are believed to dwell in the crater of Mount Apo.

BAJAU LAUT see pages 59-65

BALI AGA *Population:* small. Language group: Balinese-Sasak. The Bali Aga who live in the mountains of eastern Bali are an isolated and independent people who live in walled villages. Thought to be the pure descendants of the Indonesian Balinese, they have resisted the influence of Hinduism. However their beliefs and customs have been influenced by the more westernized peoples who surround them.

BALINESE *Population:* 2 million. Language group: Balinese-Sasak. The Balinese are predominantly farmers who grow rice, yams, sweet potatoes, cassava, and maize and coffee for export. They also rear cattle. The Balinese are famous for the sophistication and complexity of their arts – their music, dance, drama, painting and sculpture. They practise a form of Hinduism and every village has at least three elaborately carved and decorated temples: the 'origin temple' (ancestral), the 'great council temple' and the 'death temple'. Each village, with its own independent irrigation system, is organized by a *bandjar* or hamlet association of heads of households, who ensure justice, collect taxes and carry out all ritual duties.
(pages 110-123)

BANDA ISLANDERS *Population:* 20,000. Language group: Moluccan Malay. The ten Banda Islands lie in the Banda Sea 130 miles south-east of Ambon and 70 miles south of Ceram. The islanders are of mixed racial origins – mostly descendants of Javanese, Macassarese, and people from neighboring islands – who were originally brought in by the Dutch to work as slaves in the nutmeg plantations in place of the contemporary Bandanese who refused to do so, and were either killed or banished. The islanders today grow sago, rice, maize and they also fish. They cultivate nutmeg, pepper, cloves, tapioca and fruit which they sell to Chinese and Arab merchants. Most are Christians. A colony of banished Bandanese, who alone speak the old Bandanese language, continue to live on a neighboring Kai Island (q.v.).

BANGKA ISLANDERS *Population:* 260,000. Language group: Sumatran. The Muslim inhabitants of this island just off the east coast of Sumatra are mainly immigrant Malay people. Many islanders work in the huge tin-producing industry, though most of the labor is Chinese. Rice, pepper (grown by the Chinese), gambier (for dying and tanning), coffee and coconut palms are cultivated. The few aborigine hill tribes who also live there hunt, fish and collect forest produce.

BATAK *Population:* 1 million. Language group: Sumatran. The Batak live concentrated around Lake Toba in the central part of northern Sumatra. They include the linguistic groups Singkel, Pak-Pak, Dairi, Toba, Karo and Mandheling. They are farmers who grow wet and dry rice, potatoes, taro, yams, coffee, tobacco and cinnamon. Today they also plant rubber and aromatic benzoin trees. They raise cattle and horses – which are famous in the Karo highlands. In their large fortified villages they build houses with saddle-backed roofs; the fronts lean out sharply and are decorated with three lines of painted carvings in which traditional subjects are ingenuously mixed with modern ones such as pictures of Europeans and motor cars. There are cultural differences between the Batak groups. The Karo, for instance, live in long houses while the Toba do not. But there are many common Hindu elements in all their cultures.

BATJAN ISLANDERS *Population:* 30,000. Language group: Sula-Batjan. The people of this mountainous island of the Moluccas are thought to have originated from Halmahera (q.v.), and have strong affinities with the Halmahera islanders. Other inhabitants include the Serani, who are Christian descendants of Portuguese, Macassarese (q.v.), Malays and Halmaherans. And there are also some Arabs (q.v.) and Chinese (q.v.). The islanders cultivate the land on a small scale, fish, collect forest produce and make baskets. Many work on the plantations of the Batjan Exploitation Company.

BATU ISLANDERS *Population:* 17,000. Language group: Sumatran. The Batu archipelago stretches between the Nias (q.v.) and Mentawei Islands (q.v.) off western Sumatra. The islanders mostly originate from Nias, though there are some Malays (q.v.) living in the coastal towns. The Batu have a culture similar to the southern Nias (pages 76-83). They eat sago and a little rice and trade copra and forest produce. Some islanders work as goldsmiths, ironsmiths and as house builders.

BELU *Population:* 200,000. Language group: Ambon-Timor. The Belu live in central and eastern Timor. They are wealthier than their Atoni (q.v.) neighbors, as the tobacco they cultivate is in great demand all over Timor. Maize, their staple food, is supplemented with sorghum. The Belu live in oblong houses with rounded ends, and breed horses as pack animals and water buffalo (a mark of social standing).

BIKOL *Population:* 2,110,000. Language group: Bikol. The Bikol who live in south-eastern Luzon are mostly farmers. They live in villages where they grow wet rice and several fruits and vegetables including sweet potatoes, cassava, taro, beans and onions. They also cultivate coconuts and Manila hemp as cash crops. Some Bikol work in the timber industry and in the recently established mining industry, where they mine gold, silver, copper and lead.

BILLITON ISLANDERS *Population:* 110,000. Language group: Malay and Chinese dialects. This Sumatran island lies between Bangka Island and Borneo. The islanders are predominantly coastal Malays and Chinese. The aborigines (Muslims, but retaining some earlier beliefs) are related to those of Bangka Island (q.v.) and, though regarded as Malays, remain shifting cultivators who have a relatively undeveloped culture. They have a simple social organization which endows their headmen with little power. Much of the island's immigrant population works in the tin mines. Along the coast there are many fishermen, including the Orang Laut (q.v.) or sea gypsies.

BIMA *Population:* 300,000. Language group: Bima-Sumba. The Bima, together with smaller groups like the Dompa, Do Donggo and Sanggua live in eastern Sumbawa, one of the Lesser Sunda Islands. Unlike the Malayan Sumbawans (q.v.) who live in the west of the island the Bima have strong Papuan characteristics. They are shifting cultivators who grow dry upland rice, beans and tubers. Some grow coffee in the highlands. Most are Muslim.

BODHA *Population:* 4,000. Language group: Balinese-Sasak. The Bodha live in scattered settlements in the hills on Lombok, one of the lesser Sunda Islands to the east of Bali. Like the Badui (q.v.) of Java they are probably descendants of earlier inhabitants of their island. Although nominally Muslim they retain many of their original pagan beliefs.

BONFIA see CERAMESE

BONTOC IGOROT *Population:* 32,500. Language group: Bontoc. The Bontoc Igorot live between the jungle of the eastern valleys and the barren grassland of the western mountains in the north of Luzon Island. They build stone terraces where they grow wet rice, but also practise shifting cultivation of sweet potatoes, yams, and other root crops. They live in compact villages which are divided into wards, each one with a men's house, ceremonial center and a girls' sleeping place. Chiefly non-Christian their Lumawig cult tells about a miraculous person who taught the people useful arts and then ascended to become a powerful spirit.

BUGINESE
see MACASSARESE-BUGINESE

BUKIDNON *Population:* 70,000. Language group: Bukidnon. The Bukidnon live in the northern part of the Philippine island of Mindanao. Many have accepted the ways of the migrant Cebuano-speaking population and now live among them as subsistence farmers or work as farmhands on their plantations and cattle ranches. But others continue to follow their traditional way of life as *caingineros*, simple shifting cultivators, in the more remote areas. They are now a minority in their own homeland, but in two respects they remain unique: the colorful elaborately decorated dress of both sexes and their complex religious beliefs. Trained groups of men and women, although not mediums, cope with their religious ceremonies and the enormous number of spirits in which they believe.

BURU ISLANDERS *Population:* 35,000. Language groups: Ambon-Timor, Chinese Arabic. On Buru, the third largest island of the Moluccas west of Java, the indigenous population, the Alfur (inlanders) grow sago and hunt wild pigs and deer. Some villages also cultivate coconut plantations. On the coast the people who are mostly Muslims from surrounding islands together with Chinese and Arabs grow millet and manufacture cajeput oil. The Alfur abandon their inland *kampongs* (villages) if there is too much illness or bad luck and move towards the coast.

CERAMESE *Population:* 110,000. Language group: Ambon-Timor. The large Moluccan island of Ceram lies between Buru (q.v.) and New Guinea. The islanders who live in the coastal regions are people from Java (q.v.), Macassar and Ternate. They are farmers who grow rice, maize, sugar cane, tobacco and fruits. The indigenous population of the island live in several groups: the Patasiwa, once fierce head-hunters, in the west; the peace-loving Seti Patalima in the center; the Bonfia in the east. They all gather wild sago from trees and they fish and hunt with bow and arrow, *parang* (a large heavy slashing knife) and lance. They build their houses on piles off the ground and excel at making woven and plaited goods and weapons. They have largely retained their indigenous religious beliefs.

CHINESE *Population:* 6,500,000. Chinese dialects. The 3,200,000 Chinese who live in the more developed western states of the Malay peninsula are nearly all urban. They form about 37 per cent of the population. The majority work in the tin mines and plantations, though they also dominate local commerce. In Singapore nearly three quarters of the population are Chinese, and are responsible for turning the port into the prosperous center it is today. The Philippines have only about 300,000 Chinese. Many are traders and financiers. They have aroused animosity among the Filipinos because many are illegal immigrants and refuse to give up their Chinese way of life. In Indonesia many of the Chinese were expelled by President Sukarno in 1959. Those that remain, forming two per cent of the population, run small businesses, farm, or work in the tin mines and plantations.

DAYAKS see IBAN and LAND DAYAKS

DO DONGGO see BIMA

DOMPA see BIMA

ENGGANO *Population:* small. Language group: Sumatran. Enggano is a tiny island west of southern Sumatra. The indigenous inhabitants live in villages of round houses built on piles raised six to twenty feet off the ground. For food they grow taro, coconuts, yams and bananas, and also fish. Like the Mentawei (q.v.) islanders they believe in nature spirits, souls and ghosts.

HALMAHERA ISLANDERS *Population:* 70,000. Language group: North Halmahera and Malayo-Polynesian dialects. Halmahera is a large Moluccan island lying west of New Guinea. The indigenous population, the Alfur (inlander) probably originated from Papua, but have mixed with Malay peoples. They grow rice and extract wild sago from palm groves in the marshy valleys. The men also fish, dive for pearls, collect forest produce and hunt often far from home. Their villages of one family octagonal houses are built round a temple and square. In the south the Halmahera speak a Malayo-Polynesian dialect, but the language of the northern Halmahera is related to the Papuan languages of New Guinea.

IBAN *Population:* 262,000. Language group: Malay. The Iban or Sea Dayaks live around the headwaters of the Kapuas river in Indonesian Borneo, and in the hills and on the lower and middle river courses of Sarawak. They are the most energetic colonists of Borneo, having fairly recently come from Sumatra. They are very adaptable and their culture is relatively egalitarian: men of lowly rank may rise to prominence as war leaders. They are slightly built, with small bones and fine features. Originally dry rice cultivators by the slash-and-burn method in the hills, large numbers of them have turned to the easier cultivation of wet rice and cash crops such as rubber. They also hunt for food. They build their homes, long houses, usually shared by 10 to 20 families along the riverbanks. They are skilled boatmen who make long voyages to the coast. **(pages 84-91)**

IFUGAO *Population:* 80,000. Language group: Ifugao. The Ifugao, including the Inibaloi group, live along the Podis range and on the slopes of the Cordillera in the north of Luzon Island. They work in groups to build and maintain the dams and ditches for their system of rice terraces, which is the most extensive in the world. They also grow sweet potatoes, beans, corn and peas. Their activities include wood-carving, basketry and weaving as well as hunting, trapping and fishing. They raise pigs and chickens for their numerous rituals and the sacrifices that they make to over a thousand deities. They live in small scattered settlements of eight to ten houses, often perched on steep hilltops. In the past they were head hunters, and exhibited enemies' heads and feet on poles during three day village feasts.

ILOCANO *Population:* 2 million. Language group: Iloko. The Ilocano live in northern Luzon, Philippines, on a narrow coastal strip, over 160 miles long, facing the south China Sea. Apart from wet rice they also cultivate small fields of sugar cane, sweet potatoes, corn and maguey. The coastal Ilocano are fishermen, while in the towns the chief industry is pottery-making. They often wear traditional hats made from bottle gourds and shirts of traditional pattern woven on Ilocano looms. Most of their pagan practices and beliefs have disappeared. American schools, games and politics have had a greater influence than centuries of Spanish domination. Recently thousands of Ilocano have moved to other parts of Luzon. A hardworking and thrifty people, most of the Filipinos who have emigrated to America have been Ilocano.

INDIANS AND PAKISTANIS *Population:* 1,040,000. Various Indian languages. While there are about one million Indians and Pakistanis in Malaya, it is difficult to estimate their numbers in the Indonesia islands. Probably they number about 30 to 40 thousand. Most come from the Tamil, Telugu or Malayalam-speaking peoples of south India; there are also many Punjabis and Bengalis. In Malaya they were brought in to work for the early rubber plantations where most of them remain. Today an increasing number work in mines and on the railways and wharfs. Other Indian immigrants work as doctors, lawyers and in white collar jobs. In north Borneo about 2,000 are general and textile merchants in the cities and others work in the oil fields of Brunei. Most are Hindus.

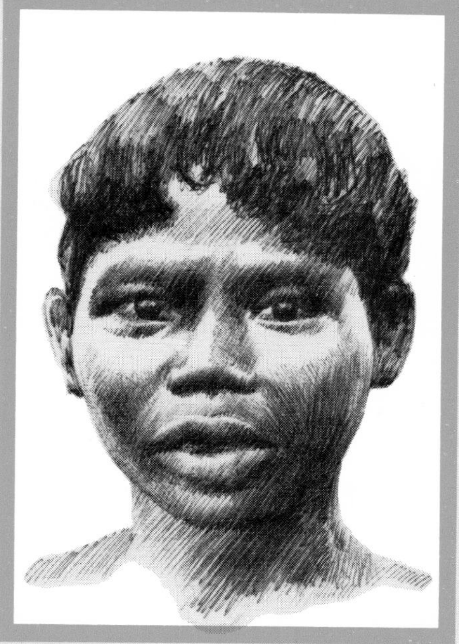

JAKUN *Population:* 20,000. Language group: Malay. The Jakun are remnants of the earliest influx of peoples of a Malay type. They are now confined to small scattered clearings in the deep jungles of eastern and southern Malaya. They hunt and fish for much of their food using blowpipes and poisoned darts. Each settlement has a headman who leads the hunt. They are pagan, unschooled and administratively regarded as aborigines like the Temiar (q.v.), Senoi (q.v.) and Negritos (q.v.).

JAVANESE *Population:* 45 million. Language group: Javanese. People who speak Javanese occupy about two-thirds of Java. In the east are numerous enclaves of migrant Madurese (q.v.), and in the west Sundanese (q.v.). Broad stretches of rice paddy, alternating with small tree-covered islands of dry land where the houses are clustered together, are criss-crossed by paved roads and paths which lead to the towns. From the earliest times Javanese culture was centered in the towns where the royal courts were held. Each village community has a communal shrine and graveyard, where the villagers hold an annual ceremony to purify the village from evil spirits. The central ritual for the Muslim Javanese, particularly the peasant, is a simple ceremonial meal called the *slametan* at which various foods are presented to the spirits. The ceremony is attended by all immediate neighbors and symbolizes one of the most deeply-felt Javanese values – mutual helpfulness and harmony among neighbors. Today town based political parties are altering the structure of rural life.
(pages 100-109)

KAI ISLANDS *Population:* 20,000. Language group: Ambon-Timor. The Moluccan Kai Islands lie in the Banda Sea to the west of the Aru Islands (q.v.). The small indigenous population the Alfur (inlanders) (q.v.) hunt and fish and grow sago which requires little or no cultivation.

KAKANAI *Population:* 91,000. Language group: Kakanai. The Kakanai live on the western slopes of the Malayan range in the north of Luzon Island. For a long time they lived in villages in the lofty highlands and grew root crops, but since the 18th century they have been building terraces where they grow wet rice. For many years they have been copper-mining, gold-panning and trading with the people of the western lowlands.

KALINGAS *Population:* 47,000. Language group: Kalinga. The Kalingas live right across the northern highlands on the island of Luzon. As well as growing sweet potatoes, taro, sugar cane (for wine), indian corn and fruit, they rear pigs, water buffalo and cattle. In the north they hunt wild pigs and deer with dogs. The Kalingas have long been famous as excellent makers of spears and axes, made today from discarded automobile springs. Few are Christians and they believe in mediums who frequently act as entertainers as well. Today an increasing number of Kalingas are moving to the towns to work for wages.

KAYAN *Population:* 25,000. Language group: Kayan. The Kayan are the most powerful inland tribe in Borneo. Historically they were the fiercest warriors and have only recently been outstripped by the Iban (q.v.) in the colonization of new land. They live in the upland regions of the Kajan, Rajang, Mahakan and Kapuas river systems as well as the Baram basin in Borneo (Kalimantan) and Sarawak. The Kayan language is the most widespread in Borneo and its four dialects are mutually intelligible. The Kayan are hunters and cultivate dry rice and sago by slash-and-burn methods. They live in long houses which are always built at the confluence of a side stream (for drinking water) and a main navigable river. Many are skilled blacksmiths and are famous for their fine craftmanship. They use the *usid kayan*, a short knife, now also used by all the other tribes of Sarawak, for all delicate work from trimming rattan to carving designs. A journey of any distance is by dugout canoe, since travel through dense forest is difficult and was formerly hazardous for all but war parties. They have a highly stratified social structure and recognize three classes, the highest being chiefs and their families.
(pages 124-131)

KELABIT *Population:* 10,000. Language group: Bornean. The Kelabit people live in the north central highlands of Borneo at the head-waters of the Baram river. They are the only Bornean hill people who have extensive irrigation systems for their rice. Many use the blow-pipe and poison dart for hunting, but hunt increasingly rarely as game is becoming more and more scarce. The Kelabit are one of the most energetic and physically well developed peoples of Borneo. They are great walkers and carry loads of up to 150 lbs for great distances along tiny jungle tracks.

KENYAH *Population:* 40,000. Language group: Bornean. The Kenyah and numerous other groups including the Murek, Ukit, Long Glat, Segai, Tring, Uma Pagong, Uma

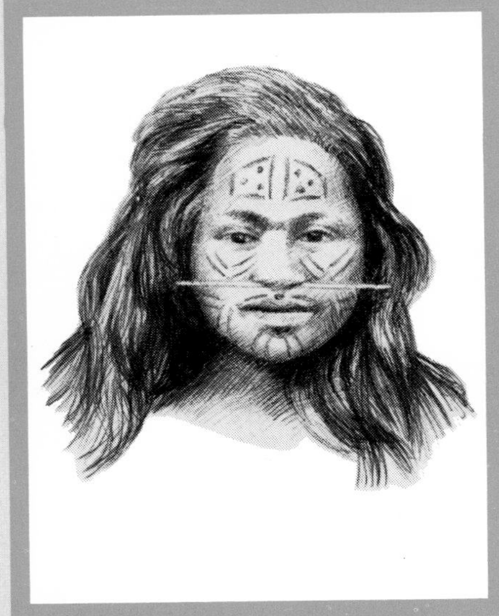

Suling, and Kayan (q.v.) live in the mountainous area of central Borneo and Sarawak. All these tribes live by growing rice and maize by slash-and-burn methods, as well as by hunting and gathering jungle produce. The Kenyah live in long houses and at Long Nawang, the great Kenyah center in the interior of Borneo, 18,000 people live in a township of over 60 huge long houses. They are among the finest artists in Borneo. The only means of travel through the dense jungle is on foot or by dugout canoe. The Kenyah who live on the Bahan river on the Sarawak border face a six week journey by dugout to the coastal bazaars to trade. They and all the other tribes in the area have a warlike past, which is still reflected in their traditional dances held on the verandas of the long houses. To the accompaniment of *sapi* (lute) music, the men dance a graceful hunt or war mime wearing bearskin war cloaks with hornbill feather headdresses. Women dance wearing fans of hornbill feathers attached to their hands.

KUBU *Population:* small. Language group: Sumatran. This small semi-nomadic group, divided into several tribes, live in swampy areas near watercourses in south-east Sumatra. They live in settlements of some 20 to 30 frail houses. The only contact they have with their neighbors is through silent trade. They place goods for barter in a place where traders can look them over and then retire. The traders thereupon put down what they are willing to give in exchange. If the deal is satisfactory the Kabu take what is offered and vanish into the bush. Forceful attempts by the Dutch to start them in settled agriculture were largely unsuccessful, but have, together with oil exploration in their territory resulted in breaking down their isolation.

KUPANGESE *Population:* 5,000. Language group: Ambon-Timor. The Kupangese live on a narrow strip of land on the south-west tip of Timor and on much of the tiny island of Semau just off it. They are shifting cultivators who use primitive tools to grow maize which they supplement with sorghum. They keep horses, cattle and water buffalo which the Kupangese consider a mark of social standing.

LAMPONG *Population:* 1 million. Language group: Sumatran. The Lampong are a group of people who live at the south-eastern end of Sumatra. They are divided into two groups: the Orang Abung or mountain people who are probably the original inhabitants, and the Orang Pablan or people of the plains who are a mixture of these and Sundanese (q.v.). The Orang Abung once hunted wild animals and gathered forest produce, but are now becoming more like the peoples of the plain who grow rice, vegetables and pepper and also fish. They live in villages of stilted houses grouped round a communal house which they build by rivers. They know nothing of Islamic law despite their nominal Mohammedanism.

LAND DAYAKS *Population:* 60,000. Language group: Bornean. The Land Dayaks are largely settled in inland areas of south-west Sarawak and Borneo. They are one of the two main indigenous groups in Borneo and are less mongoloid than the Iban (q.v.) or Sea Dayaks, and include many tribes. They practise slash-and-burn dry rice agriculture, although some groups also grow wet rice. They have an elaborate system of labor exchange between families, and keep a rigorous account of labor credits and debts. They build their villages of one or more long houses on river bends. In each village there is a headhouse which serves as a guest house, the men's meeting place and the bachelors' sleeping quarters. In the past headhunting trophies were also displayed in the headhouse.

LARANTUKA see SIKA

LETI ISLAND *Population:* 20,000. Language group: Ambon-Timor. Lakor, Kisor and Moa are the main Leti Islands which lie east of Timor. The indigenous population, the Alfur (inlander) fish and hunt for food. Their staple crop, sago, needs little or no cultivation.

LINGGA-RIOUW ISLANDERS *Population:* 280,000. Language group: Riouw Malay. The Lingga-Riouw archipelago lies to the east of Sumatra just south of Malaya. The people are Malays (q.v.), Buginese (see Macassarese-Buginese) and Chinese (q.v.). The Malays and Buginese live by simple agriculture and fishing and cultivate rubber and copra as cash crops. The Chinese grow pepper and gambier (a product used mainly for tanning) and exploit the forests for timber, firewood and charcoal. Many work in the tin mines of Singkep and the bauxite mines on Bintan. The islanders are nearly all Muslim. The few aborigines are still nomadic hunters and gatherers, using the bow, arrow and poisoned dart. They live in rude shelters of bamboo and leaves.

LIONESE see NGADA

LOINANG *Population:* 200,000. Language

group: Loinang. The Loinang group of peoples live in the eastern limb and adjacent offshore islands of Sulwasi. The group includes the Balantak, Banggai and Wana. They are farmers who grow rice, maize, cassava, yams and beans, and copra and spices for export. They also collect various forest products and excel at weaving and plaiting fibers. They are nearly all Muslim.

LONG GLAT see KENYAH

MACASSARESE-BUGINESE *Population:* 5 million. Language group: South Celebes. This group lives in south-western Celebes (Sulwasi), the two million Macassarese in the southern part and over three million Buginese mostly in the north. Historically, they are one of the most active Muslim seafaring peoples of the East Indies, who acquired great notoriety as pirates and slavers. Now some are inter-island traders, but most are farmers and craftsmen. Their chief crop is wet rice, but they also grow maize. Their main industry is weaving. They live in pile-dwellings grouped in villages of 20 to 40 families. Buginese colonies are found all along the coast of Celebes, as well as Borneo, Bali (q.v.) and Lombok. The Macassarese have rituals for sacred ornaments carried out by non-Islamic priests called *bissu*, while the Buginese have become strict Muslims.

MADURESE *Population:* 5 million. Language group: Javanese. About half the Madurese live on the island of Madura, which adjoins north-east Java; the rest have emigrated to eastern Java. The islanders cultivate Madura's poor soil to the utmost. Rice is a great luxury and maize forms the basis of their diet. They also export teak, copra and coconut oil. Many raise cattle and work in the large government-monopolized salt industry.

MALAYS *Population:* 10 million. Language group: Malay. The five million Malays who live in the Malaya peninsula are primarily rural, though they are increasingly moving to the towns. They live in stilted houses in spread-out villages where they grow wet rice. They also work in the rubber, coconut and pineapple exporting industries. Many are involved in cattle rearing, forestry and mining, especially for iron ore.
The 2,300,000 Malay who live in the eastern half of Sumatra are mostly shifting cultivators who grow poor quality wet rice. They are good sailors who have ventured all over the archipelago.
In Borneo there are about 700,000 Malays who live in the coastal areas particularly in the sultanates of Brunei and Sambas. They have intermarried extensively with the Javanese (q.v.), Buginese (see Macassarese-Buginese) and Arabs (q.v.). Inland they live in simple villages and grow dry rice or in raft villages and travel up the southern rivers to trade with the Dayak peoples (see Iban and Land Dayak). The coastal Malays are fishermen.

MANDAYA *Population:* 35,000. Language group: Mandaya. The Mandaya live on both slopes of the rough mountain range that borders the Pacific Ocean, in the southern part of the Philippine island of Mindanao. They live in houses built in the trees and grow scanty crops of dry rice, tobacco and cotton. The men hunt and the women gather jungle fruits and roots. They are considered the most warlike of the Filipino peoples but most have now been pacified by Christian settlers and government control. Both sexes traditionally wear embroidered jackets to which they attach silver disks.

MANGGARAI *Population:* 320,000. Language group: Bima-Sumba. The Manggarai live in western Flores, one of the Lesser Sunda Islands, lying between Sumbawa (q.v.) and Solor. They have more Malay characteristics than the other groups living on the island. They are shifting cultivators who grow maize and root crops. They use only sticks to turn over the soil. Many hunt and fish in their densely forested, mountainous territory. Their houses, often built on piles, are surrounded by a bamboo hedge and are round with high conical roofs

which reach down to the ground. Sometimes a whole village will live in one or two communal houses.

MANGYANS *Population:* 20,000. Language group: Mangyan. Mangyans is a collective name for several groups who live in the forested uplands in the interior of Mindoro Island, Philippines. They are subsistence farmers who grow upland rice. They also hunt and gather forest produce. They have little contact with the Christian people of the lowlands.

MELANAU *Population:* 60,000. Language group: Bornean, Malay. The Melanau live on the lower reaches and deltas of the rivers in Sarawak. They are skilful sailors and builders and the most successful fishermen in Sarawak. They also harvest huge plots of wild sago which they bake into round 'sago pearls' to eat and to trade. They live in individual houses built along the river banks. They believe in spirits, *belum* who cause illness and *bayuh* who cure illness. They build carved wooden memorial pillars where they place burial jars at a great ceremony.

MENTAWEI ISLANDERS *Population:* 30,000. Language group: Sumatran. Siberut is the largest of the Mentawei Islands which lie west of central Sumatra. The islanders grow taro, bananas, sugar cane and coconut, apart from their staple crop, sago. They hunt and fish for much of their food supply. They hunt deer and monkeys with dogs and the bow and poisoned arrow. Their villages are built on inland streams and are divided into wards each with its own pile-built communal house. They have a national drink, *djurut*, made with coconut milk, sugar cane sap, sliced bananas and the meat of young coconuts. They worship the spirits of animals.

MINAHASA *Population:* 1,700,000. Language groups: Minahasa, Gorontalo. The Minahasa live in the eastern half of the northern peninsula of Celebes. Late in the 19th century Dutch coffee planters and missionaries arrived and Minahasa society was totally transformed, within several decades, from a head-hunting tribal group to a settled peasant economy, based primarily on cash crops and with a Christian and highly westernized culture. The people now cultivate rice, coconuts, coffee and spices on the fertile soil of the island. Because of the excellent missionary schools, many people are highly educated. Like the Ambonese (q.v.), Minahasa hold important positions in the civil service in Indonesia.

MINANGKABAU *Population:* 1,500,000. Language group: Sumatran. The Minangkabau live in the western coastlands and highlands of central Sumatra. On steep, mountainside fields they grow dry rice, millet, sugar cane, beans, corn, tobacco and even cabbages. They rear buffalo, horses and goats, and horned cattle (which they trade). Their chief industries are spinning, weaving, lace-making and the preparation of silk. Many are now successful businessmen who export rubber, coffee and coconuts, and are astute enough to cut out the Chinese merchants as middlemen in Minangkabau towns. Their beautifully carved houses in the towns bear witness to their prosperity. Their religion is a mixture of Hindu and Islam, with their original beliefs.

MORI-LAKI *Population:* 230,000. Language group: Bungku-Laki. The Mori-Laki group of peoples live in the southwestern peninsula, and the islands of Kabaena, Wowoni and Butung, adjacent to Sulwasi (Celebes). They are primarily farmers, growing rice, maize, coconuts and tobacco, and they collect food from the forest. They process copra for export, and weave and plait. Most of the Mori-Laki are Muslims.

MOROS *Population:* 1 million. Language group: Moro. The Moro peoples live on the Philippine island of Mindanao and several other islands to the south. There are several groups, including the Sulu, Samal, Magindanao, Lanao and Maranao, each with its own language, traditional territory and customs. They are essentially a people who live by the water, by fishing, pearl-fishing and even by smuggling and piracy. Some islanders build their homes on piles over the sea. All are at home in the slender canoes they once used on pirate raids. On the land they grow rice, and are skilled metal-workers, particularly the Maranao, who make brassware and weapons. When the Spanish invaded the island the people were already largely converted to Islam.
(pages 50-53)

MUREK see KENYAH

MURUT *Population:* 15,000. Language group: Bornean. The Murut live in north central Borneo in the Trusan river valley, although much of the tribe has moved from the hilly inaccessible interior to coastal districts. With the Kelabit (q.v.) they are among the most productive wet rice planters in Sarawak. They also engage in the shifting cultivation of sweet potatoes, manioc, and maize. They fish, hunt, and collect forest produce, including rattan. Their rapidly disappearing long houses often have a remarkable sprung dance floor mounted on curved saplings, which may hold as many as thirty dancers jumping rhythmically and singing.

NEGRITOS *Population:* a few thousand. Language group: Austro-asiatic or Negrito. The Negritos are of a true pygmy stock found, in isolated remnants, deep in the jungle in parts of Indonesia, the Philippines and Malaya (eg the Semang, q.v.). They live in the mountainous parts of eastern and western Luzon, in the upland interiors of Panay and Negros islands, in north-east Mindanao, and in upland northern Palawan.

They hunt small game with bows and arrows and with blowpipes and collect forest produce. At the time of the Spanish infiltration into the Philippines they were already restricted to the upland forest areas. Today their numbers are declining in the Philippines, and probably elsewhere.

NGADA *Population:* 300,000. Language group: Bima-Sumba. The Ngada, together with the Lionese, live in much of western and central Flores, one of the lesser Sunda Islands, which lies between Sumbawa and Solor. They are farmers who grow maize and root crops. They hunt and fish to supplement their diet. Their houses, often round and built on piles, are divided into separate rooms to house each family. Each village has its barns and sometimes the *pemali* house, where pagan offerings are made and relics are kept. Chiefs have large herds of roaming cattle.

NIAS *Population:* 250,000. Language group: Sumatran. The island of Nias, 650 square miles, lies just west of Sumatra in the Indian Ocean. The islanders are mostly farmers, though on the north coast they catch and eat a lot of fish. There are linguistic, political and social differences between northern and southern Nias. The southern villages are large and well laid out, with an abundant water supply while in the north they are small and depend on natural features to conceal and protect them. The Nias mined copper as early as the 10th century and gold probably long before. Every village has a stone bench, originally erected as a seat for the ghosts of the dead, under which the Nias keep the skulls of their ancestors.
(pages 76-83)

ORANG ABUNG see LAMPONG

ORANG LAUT Generally regarded as proto-Malays, unlike the Jakun (q.v.) who retreated into the jungles, the Orang Laut took refuge, and survived on remote islands and sea shores. The Orang Laut or sea gypsies live scattered along the coast from Burma to Borneo, but they are especially numerous in the Riau archipelago off the southern tip of Malaya. As long as the weather permits they live at sea in boats, together with their dogs and chickens. During the stormy season they build shelters on the shore and live on shell fish. Some have settled permanently in the marshy lands around the Inderagiri river in south-east Sumatra, and on adjacent islands. They cultivate plantations of coconut and many are nominally Muslim.

ORANG PABLAN see LAMPONG

PAMPANGAN *Population:* 642,000. Language group: Kapampangan. These Filipino people live in the heart of the central plain on the island of Luzon in a region extending northward from Manila Bay and drained by the Pampanga river. Many of them are tenant farmers or work as farm laborers. They grow mainly rice and sugar cane, and also fish and manufacture nipan palm products. They have retained much of their own distinctive culture, despite their closeness to Manila.

PANGASINAN *Population:* 520,000. Language group: Pangasinan. The indigenous Pangasinan live in the central area of Pangasinan province on the Philippine island of Luzon. They are farmers who grow rice, maize, mangoes, sugar, tobacco and coconut. The Pangasinan intermarry frequently with their numerous Ilocano (q.v.) neighbors. Most are Roman Catholic, but some belong to the Philippine Independent Church, a breakaway movement from Catholicism that originated in the rebellion against Spain, in 1663.

PATALIMA see CERAM

PATASIWA see CERAM

PATASIWA PUTIH see CERAM

PENAN *Population:* 4,000. Language group: Bornean. The Penan group of peoples live in the jungle-covered mountains in the interior of Sarawak and Borneo. They are nomads who roam the forest in search of wild sago palms. They are skilled trackers and hunt wild pigs, deer, monkeys, clouded leopards and black honey bears with poisonous darts blown from blowpipes. They build temporary shelters of branches wherever they find sago, only moving on when the sago is all gone, or after 15 days have elapsed or if somebody dies. When moving camp the men forage ahead while the women and children follow at a more leisurely pace. Once slaves of the

Kayan (q.v.) and Kenyah (q.v.) the Penan are now used as porters by these tribes to carry baskets of rice and other foods along jungle trails to the nearest navigable point on the rivers.

REDJANG *Population:* 180,000. Language group: Sumatran. The Redjang live in the highlands and foothills of the Barisan mountain range in south-west Sumatra. They practise upland slash-and-burn dry-rice cultivation, and many are fishermen. For centuries their country has been a magnet for seekers of mineral wealth, especially gold. Nominally Muslim, every Redjang village has at least one shaman or medicine man. They export their annual rice surplus, and by Sumatran standards are a prosperous people.

ROTINESE *Population:* 70,000. Language group: Ambon-Timor. The Rotinese live on the small island of Roti which lies four miles from the south-west tip of Timor. They are wet-rice farmers but earn additional money by fishing, salt making, charcoal burning, collecting bebak and lime, and lontar tapping. In the island's harsh environment the lontar palm has been called the Rotinese 'tree of life'. It provides several foods and drinks, raw materials for numerous consumer goods and the Rotinese have been exporting lontar sugar and syrup for many years.

SAMAL LAUT *Population:* 120,000. Language group: Samal. Samal Laut refers to several groups of peoples, also called Balangingi, who live on the Sulu archipelago which stretches from the southern end of the Philippines to the coast of northern Borneo. They like to live on boats or in boat-and-shore environments, and depend on the sea for their livelihood. These people are the 'sea gypsies' proper, since other groups like the shore Samal and Bajau (see pages 59-65) have become less mobile. Though they collect many marine products – sponges, pearls, coral, shark fins and turtle eggs, they do grow a little rice, cassava and corn. In fact most families now claim a house or a village ashore, even though they may spend much time away. They still make their traditional boats and their highly developed bronze and iron tools: they work in many metals. They had accepted Islam by the 18th century. They refuse to be bound by patterns of modern political nationalism, tariff-boundaries and immigration regulations, and many are still smugglers.

SANGGAU see BIMA

SASAK *Population:* 1 million. Language group: Balinese-Sasak. The population of Lombok, one of the Lesser Sunda Islands, is largely Sasak, who are the indigenous inhabitants. The influence of the Balinese, formerly their overlords, is apparent, although the Sasaks are culturally on a much lower level. Their elaborately organized agriculture – they grow sweet potatoes, coffee, coconuts and tobacco – includes an excellent irrigation system. They weave clothes and mats. Some work in gold, silver and iron. They are nominally Muslim, but lax in their observances. One large group of Sasak eat pork and drink strong liquor.

SEGAI see KENYAH

SEMANG *Population:* 3,000. Language group: Austro-asiatic. The Semang are Negritos (q.v.) who live in the jungles of Malaya. Groups have been encountered as far south as Pahang, but most are probably in Kelantan, Perak and Kedah or across the Thai border. They are small bands of negroid pygmies, mostly nomadic, occasionally attaching themselves to more secure aboriginal groups such as the Temiar (q.v.). They are rarely contacted by outsiders. They live in leaf shelters and eat jungle fruits and animals which they hunt with bows and arrows and blowpipes. They trap, spear or poison fish with the juice from tuber roots.

SENOI *Population:* 30,000. Language group: Senoi and Senoi-Temiar. The Senoi or Sakai (strangers) is a name given by Malays to several groups of aborigines living in remote forest clearings in the central mountain area of the Malay peninsula. They include the Temiar (q.v.). Perhaps derived from an early mixing of the most ancient inhabitants of this area, the Negritos (q.v.) and proto-Malays (see Jakum), they practise a simple agriculture clearing and burning the land to grow rice, millet, tapioca, bananas and tobacco. They raise a few chickens and pigs mainly to trade with up-river Malays by whom they are sometimes harshly exploited. During the Malayan emergency of the 1950s British and Malay forces employed Senoi as guides because of their remarkable powers of jungle navigation and survival.

SETI see CERAMESE

SIKA *Population:* 100,000. Language group: Bima-Sumba. The Sika live in parts of eastern Flores, one of the Lesser Sunda Islands lying between Sumbawa (q.v.) and Solor. The inhabitants of Larantuka, largely descended from the Portuguese and the Badjawanese also populate east Flores. They are a mixed, enterprising people, mostly shifting cultivators who grow coconuts along the coast and export copra. Their houses are small and for one family only. Some Sika are also fishermen and hunters.

SUMBANESE *Population:* 260,000. Language group: Bima-Sumba. The Sumbanese live on Sumba, one of the Lesser Sunda Islands lying south of Flores. Apart from the indigenous Sumbanese there are many people who have settled there from surrounding islands. The Sumbanese themselves speak several different languages and the tribes in the west are more primitive than the rest, including scattered groups of Negritos. The islanders grow rice, coffee, coconuts, tobacco, vegetables and fruit and they breed fine horses and cattle. Though some are Muslims, most retain their original beliefs. Polygamy is common among the upper classes.

SUMBAWANS *Population:* 200,000. Language group: Balinese-Sasak. The Sumbawans live in the western half of Sumbawa, one of the Lesser Sunda Islands lying between Lombok and Flores. Unlike the Bima (q.v.) in the east of the island the people are of Malay stock, and they speak a different language. They raise many types of field vegetables and root crops together with cotton and sugar cane. They grow many tree crops such as lontar palm and citrus fruits. They rear horses, water buffalo, goats, chickens and ducks. The densest population lives in the wet rice growing river valleys. For the last 400 years they have been dominated in one way or another by the Macassarese (q.v.), who originally brought Islam to Sumbawa.

SUNDANESE *Population:* 10 million. Language group: Javanese. The Sundanese live chiefly in the western area of Java, in the Priangan Highlands, which is the center of their territory. Originally hill peoples, they are the second largest ethnic group in Indonesia. They cultivate both wet and dry rice, and are strongly Muslim. Their culture is similar to that of the Javanese (q.v.); many are among the Javan urban élite. An increasing number are becoming wage earners.

TAGAL *Population:* 10,000. Language group: Bornean. The Tagal live in the most mountainous part of Sarawak, in Salah near Pensiangan. Like the Murut (q.v.) they are wet rice cultivators and hunters. They are also known as the 'north Borneo Murut' and live in very much the same way, although they speak their own dialect. Many are now Christians or more recently converted Muslims.

TAGALOG *Population:* 3,800,000. Language group: Tagalog. These Filipino people live in and around the capital Manila, on the island of Luzon. Most are farmers whose *sitios* (small hamlets) are clustered together with surrounding farmlands. Their rice, mostly wet, but dry in the upland areas, is eaten locally, and they also grow sugar cane and coconut for export. Many urban Tagalog work in middle class occupations such as banking and commerce in Manila. They are highly literate and have led in the modernization of the Philippines. The second largest ethnic group, Tagalog is by law the national language.

TANIMBAR ISLANDERS *Population:* 50,000. Language group: Ambon-Timor. This group of islands is in the south-east Moluccas to the south-west of the Aru islands. The islanders are of Papuan stock although there has been much mixture with mongoloid strains of the Indonesian and Malay type. They cultivate maize, yams, rice, coconut and sago palms and plantains. The men are skilful boat builders, use the spear and bow and arrow to shoot fish, hunt, search for trepang (sea cucumbers) and turtle shells. They keep pigs and work in iron, copper and gold. The women cultivate the fields. Although some are Muslims and Christians, they have largely retained their original beliefs.

TASADAY *Population:* under 30. The Tasaday live in a small group isolated in the forest which covers the southern highlands of Mindanao Island. They do not build houses but live in caves on cliff faces. They eat wild yams, bananas, grubs and pith from young palm trees and collect tadpoles, frogs and little fish from streams. They smoke the meat of deer, mice and monkeys which they occasionally trap, in order to preserve it. The Tasaday have no leaders and decisions are taken communally. They have few religious beliefs but fear the cries of certain birds, the harbingers of death. When a Tasaday dies his body is left in the forest covered with leaves. The outside world first knew of their existence in 1971.
(pages 38-49)

TAUSOG *Population:* 240,000. Language group: Tausog. The Tausog live on the many islands of the Sulu archipelago, the 'little sea world' at the south-western end of the Philippine Islands. They live along the shore in pile-built villages and hamlets. They farm and fish; their crops include cassava, rice, coconuts and corn. They have been Muslims since the 15th century and built principalities, political states and small sea-empires. From the 16th to the early 19th century they were traders and raiders who preyed upon the islands to the north and south. They resolutely refuse to be tied down by political boundaries and regulations, and some are smugglers.

TEMIAR (or SEMAI-TEMIAR) *Population:* several thousand. Language group: Senoi-Temiar. The Temiar live deep in the Malayan jungle, in highland Perak and Kalantan. Their usual form of dwelling is a bamboo long house, shared by the whole community, built on stilts. 'Lower strata' Temiar, living in the less healthy river valleys, such as the Nenggiri, inhabit simpler shelters more akin to the Negritos', with whom there may have been partial mixture in the distant past. Tamiar are more curly-haired than Proto-Malays, like the Jakun (q.v.), semi-nomadic, practising cultivation within certain hereditary areas, and hunting and trapping game. They were much disturbed by the Chinese communist guerilla campaign from 1947 to the late 1960's. Their chief weapon is the blowpipe; and they are highly skilled at various forms of animal traps, not least the pit traps (camouflaged holes on forest tracks, with sharpened stakes sticking upwards) and drop traps – heavily weighted and sharpened bamboo stakes, carried high into the trees and released by a rattan 'trip wire': these can kill an elephant or *seladang*. The spring trap is regarded as most dangerous to the unwary: a bent sapling which can release a spear with sufficient force to pass through a man's body. Their melodic instrument is the nose flute.

TINGUIAN *Population:* 40,000. Language group: Tinguian. The Tinguian people live mostly in large scattered villages in the Abra river basin in northern Luzon. They grow both upland and wet rice, and fish, weave and make rope and nets. They are chiefly nomadic and rural and have retained more of their traditions than surrounding groups. These include a belief in Kadaklan, 'the greatest', who lives in the sky with his dog Kimat, the lightning. They are, however, disappearing as a distinct group owing to pressures from their powerful neighbors, the Ilocano (q.v.).

TORADJA GROUP *Population:* 700,000. Language group: Bornean. This is a collective name covering many separate tribes in central, south-east and eastern Celebes (Sulwasi). They live in small, self-sufficient villages, though the Dutch forced them to move down into the valleys from their fortified hilltop settlements. They hunt, fish, gather forest produce and grow rice and maize by slash-and-burn methods. Recently they have started to cultivate irrigated rice. Their communal family houses have saddle roofs resembling those of the Toba Batak (q.v.) in Sumatra. The few Toradja industries include plaiting, pottery and wood carving. Most are Christians.

TRING see KENYAH

UKIT see KENYAH

UMA PAGONG see KENYAH

UMA SULING see KENYAH

VISAYAN *Population:* 5,400,000. Language group: Visayan. The Visayan peoples live in the Visaya Islands, the central islands of the Philippines. Though some are urban most of the Visayan live in agricultural villages where they grow both wet and dry rice, and some sweet potatoes, cassava, taro, yams and bananas. In the western islands they grow coconuts, manila hemp and sugar cane to sell. Tens of thousands of Visayan fish in the Sibuyan Sea where they catch anchovies, sardines, herring, shrimp and crab. The Philippines were under Spanish rule for more than 300 years from 1572, and the Visayan remain one of the more Spanish influenced peoples of the Philippines.

All population figures are approximate.